Elizabeth Fry

Elizabeth Fry

Friend of Prisoners

Catherine M. Swift

Marshall Pickering

Marshall Morgan and Scott
Marshall Pickering
3 Beggarwood Lane, Basingstoke, Hants RG23 7LP, UK

First published in 1986 by
Marshall Morgan and Scott Publications Ltd
Part of the Marshall Pickering Holdings Group
A subsidiary of the Zondervan Corporation

ISBN 0 551 01355 9

Text Set in Plantin by
Brian Robinson, Buckingham.
Printed in Great Britain by Hazell Watson & Viney Ltd,
Member of BPCC Group,
Aylesbury, Bucks

Contents

1: Foundation and Inspiration

Elizabeth Gurney was born into a loving, caring family. Now although that seems normal, as she was born two hundred years ago, her family was rather unusual.

Not only did they love and care for each other but for everyone – even people they didn't know or were ever likely to know. But then, they had always been good, kindhearted people.

It was in 1066, as supporters of William the Conqueror, that the 'Lords of Gournay-on-Bray' first set foot in England. Some years later, William Rufus, the conqueror's son, grateful for their loyalty to him and to his father, gave them a lot of land in Norfolk.

Nevertheless, a few of the Lords of Gournay-on-Bray returned to their Normandy homeland to stay. But others returned to England, bringing with them their wives and children to settle on their newly-acquired land in the eastern part of the country. After a while they decided to drop their full title and became known simply as the Gurneys.

Although they'd come to England as conquerors, they didn't rule harshly. From the very beginning they set out to help, not only their immediate neighbours and tenants of their land, but anyone in need.

First they went to all the small farms round about where they lived and bought up all the wool the farmers had sheared from their sheep. This they took to the poor people living in the nearby cottages and paid them to spin and weave it into cloth. When this was done, the Gurneys took it to market in Norwich, the county city of Norfolk, and there they sold it to the European wool merchants.

As the woven cloth was of far higher value than wool in its raw state, this new way of trading meant that more money was being kept in this country rather than going abroad as it had in the past.

This trading method helped Norwich to grow into the great city it is now and it also earned more money for the Gurneys themselves. They made so much money that they were able to lend it out to poor people to enable them to buy livestock, crop-seed, land, houses or businesses of their own.

The family became so well known for their honesty and trustworthiness that more and more people traded with them. Others borrowed more and more money from them, paying it back bit by bit and a little extra (interest) for the privilege of borrowing it in the first place. Almost without realising what was happening, the Gurney family had become bankers.

Many years later there was a time when England's flax crop failed and the linen weavers, who relied on it for their living, were in danger of starvation. Again it was a Gurney who came to their aid. He went to Ireland and bought up all their flax harvest. The Irish too were near starving at that time and were grateful for this unexpected trade.

When the Irish flax crop arrived in England it was sent to our weavers and spinners. Until then they'd believed there would be no work for them that year. Now they had as much as they could cope with, which kept them from starvation too.

That man was John Gurney, Elizabeth's grandfather. He died in 1770, ten years before Elizabeth was born, and he left a fortune of £100,000. That is very rich, even by today's standards. At that time it must have been more so when we consider that a man's weekly wage was but a few pence.

Another of Elizabeth's ancestors, again called John, learned that by importing woven cotton from other countries to England, not only were British people keeping work from their own weavers: they were adding to the misery of slavery. The more cotton a foreign country could sell, the more it extended its plantations to grow more cotton. It then needed more slaves to tend the bigger crops.

John Gurney was so angry at this that he went to the House of Lords to present the facts to Parliament. When he begged them to stop buying the woven cotton, he made such a good impression that they immediately had the trade stopped and asked John if he would stand for Parliament. But the Gurney family belonged to the Society of Friends, which wouldn't allow its members to become involved with politics.

The Society of Friends had been founded in Leicestershire in 1624 by a shoemaker named George Fox. He was disgusted at all the bickering that went on between people of different religious ideals. He said it was wrong for 'Christian to be against Christian' when they all believed in the same God, so he left his church to establish a doctrine of his own.

He thought people should feel free to worship God in the way they thought best. There should be no such things as churches or sacred buildings because God was everywhere. Why not just have a Meeting House where anyone could go? He would have no ministers or priests and there would be no set prayers or services. He was sure many recited prayers were impossible for uneducated people to understand.

George Fox shocked the people of England even more when he said everyone should be treated equally in his Society of Friends. Rich or poor, men and women, all were the same. No one had ever dreamed until then that women were the equal of men and should be treated with the same respect. But George couldn't accept that any one person could be more important than another. No one should be expected to bow or curtsey to another either, he said, so royalty and other high ranks were merely shown the same esteem as anyone else.

He would have no saints' days or holy days. Didn't every single day belong to the Lord? There was to be no baptism because we are all born God's children. And no communion because the Lord is already within all of us.

He disapproved of men removing their hats on entering any building as it implied that the building was sacred, and buildings couldn't be sacred, so men must keep their hats on at all times.

Fox believed that a person's aim in life was to abolish suffering and pain the world over. Yet he didn't approve of missionaries except as teachers, doctors or nurses as no one had the right to impose his religion on others. It was something people should choose for themselves.

Members of his Society should not attend University as this went against Fox's belief that everyone should receive the same education. Nor could they take up law and stand in judgement on their fellow beings. Oaths could not be taken as this implied that people were free to tell lies the rest of the time, and no one should ever lie, steal or cheat.

Fox said that war was the most wicked of all things. No one should take up arms against his fellow humans. But wherever foolish people were fighting each other, the Friends would be there to doctor the wounded and offer comfort to the dying.

Friends must never expect reward of any kind for their work because this would lead to vanity. Vanity and pride were weaknesses not to be indulged in. Fox disapproved of coloured clothes, jewellery, music and dancing. In a world full of pain and suffering such pleasures were not to be considered.

Although these rules of George Fox's new Society of Friends were meant to simplify religion and destroy all the divisions amongst Christians, they really made life more complicated. His opposition to bright clothes and jollity of any kind only made the Friends stand out from everyone else, when what he was aiming at was for them to fade into the background.

Next to war, Fox most detested slavery, and in 1676 he was the very first person to speak out against it. The Society of Friends were the first people in the world to give up the evil slave trade and the owning of slaves. And this is why it was a Gurney who went to the House of Lords to voice his objections over the import of cotton.

Even after that time, between 1680 and 1776, just four years before Elizabeth was born, two million slaves were captured and shipped from what people called 'savage' Africa to be sold in many parts of the more 'civilized' world.

For centuries, people mocked this new Society of Friends. Much fun was made of them when an eminent person of the land said, 'They become so emotional over their religion that they tremble and quake.'

From then on everyone called them Quakers. It was meant as an insult, yet, in time, as people grew accustomed to their strange ways and accepted them, Quaker became a very respectable name and is still used to this day.

2: Elizabeth's Early Childhood

By the time Elizabeth was born in 1780, her family had been Quakers for over two hundred years.

Her father, again called John Gurney, had inherited, from a relative, a wool processing factory together with a large house where he lived with his beautiful wife, Catherine. Catherine's grandfather was the founder of Barclays Bank, and as the Gurneys were also bankers, both families knew each other well. How pleased they were when John and Catherine said they wanted to marry. It was clear for all to see that they loved each other very much.

Their home stood in Magdalen Street in the heart of Norwich city. It had many long casement windows. Its doors had pointed archways over the top and, jutting out of the roof, were more windows fronting the garrets where the servants slept. It was called the Court House and is still there today. It hasn't changed much except for the archways but it is now called Gurney Court. Another difference is that it no longer looks out on to the big garden that was there when Elizabeth was born on May 21st, 1780.

John and Catherine already had two daughters, Kate and Rachel. There had been a boy, John, but he had died as a baby.

Like all her family, Elizabeth was beautiful. Her tall, slim mother with her fair skin and long golden hair was so lovely that her husband had her portrait painted. Yet Catherine's wasn't merely the kind of beauty which can be seen. It came from within her and her goodness shone out to the world through her deep, blue eyes. And Elizabeth's father, 'Handsome Johnny' as he was called, dressed in his tail-coat with long hose and knee-breeches, was thought to be the best looking man in Norfolk with his red-brown hair and laughing eyes.

Elizabeth was a miniature of her mother with golden hair and blue eyes. Kate and Rachel had the looks of their father, with dancing eyes and flame-coloured hair.

Although John and Catherine Gurney kept their faith as Quakers, they didn't observe the rules as strictly as they were expected to. After a century of persecution, when Quakers were finally accepted by everyone, many of them began to relax some of the more severe regulations. For a time they actually split into two separate groups, Plain Quakers and Wide Quakers.

True to their teachings, Plain Quakers followed George Fox's rules. They disapproved of all show of vanity by continuing to wear their dark, plain clothes without collars or buttons. They didn't sing, dance, play cards or go to the theatre. Even children were not expected to play and have fun but to dwell on all the unhappiness in the world.

Wide Quakers refused to agree to such severe conditions, and Elizabeth's parents belonged to this second group. They had both been brought up in Plain Quaker families, but once they were married they changed their ways. John wanted to take his lovely young wife to parties, balls and to the theatre. And for business reasons he wanted to associate with people who weren't Quakers at all – something which was frowned upon by the Society of Friends. This was partly due to all the persecution they had received when George Fox first established his Society. People tended to avoid these strange people with their strange ideas and, in turn, the Quakers kept well away from them. It took many generations before all Quakers could bring themselves to mingle freely with the outside world as they do now.

There was another good reason for renouncing the Plain Quaker ways. As the men were expected to keep their hats on, even in the house, it could be very embarrassing for John to enter a non-Quaker house and not remove his hat. Although he was simply observing a rule of his faith, to his host or hostess it looked like an act of downright rudeness.

And so the Gurneys wore ordinary clothes. The children studied music, dancing, played games and had birthday parties. They lived in exactly the same way all children of wealthy parents lived outside the strict Quaker faith.

Nevertheless, although John and Catherine were not strict Quakers, they were very strict parents – or tried to be. Being rich they were always giving the children all sorts of luxuries and treats, but this didn't mean they were spoiled. Their mother and father insisted on their being well behaved at all times. Unfortunately, they weren't always as good as they should have been.

By the time Elizabeth was five, as well as her two older sisters she had four younger ones and a brother. He was born the year after Elizabeth and was called John after the baby who had died some years earlier. After him came Richenda. The following year Hannah was born; a year later, Louisa arrived, followed the year after by Priscilla.

They were a lively family, full of mischief and always playing practical jokes. It was probably because there were so many of them that Elizabeth's difference went unnoticed for a long time.

Even though they had such a large house, as there were so many people living in it, the Court House simply didn't have enough room for them all, so after Priscilla was born when Elizabeth was five, the family moved from Norwich.

Their new home, Earlham, was only a short distance

from the city. It was a beautiful red-brick, ivy-covered mansion standing in its own parkland. Vast lawns ringed by massive trees had peacocks strutting about on them. The gardens sloped down to where the River Wensum flowed through the grounds. The children were used to this river because it ran close to their old home. But now part of it passed through their own land and they could play on its banks or go boating. All, that is, except Elizabeth, who was terrified of the deep water.

She was afraid of the house too, with all its space and dozens of rooms. It had winding staircases leading to numerous attics. There were lots of little rooms too, where, in days gone by, men and women had retired to powder their wigs.

Earlham had nearly one hundred cupboards, big enough for people to hide in. But, whereas the other Gurney children saw the house as being perfect for playing all sorts of games, Elizabeth was even more afraid of it than she was of the river – especially at night. She always had to have a light in her room.

Her father loved to go fishing in the river or shooting in Earlham Park. Elizabeth, or Betsy as she was called, hated this too. One day when they were all going out into the country for a picnic, she screamed and refused to get into the carriage. This was because her father was taking his gun and had put it on the seat beside him. Betsy was convinced that at the picnic he would become like Abraham and sacrifice her like Isaac.

She was so afraid of everything, the river, the sea, loud bangs – she would even jump at her own shadow. The other children were often irritated by her and teased her. This made her very shy and quiet. At other times they would feel sorry for her because she missed all the fun that they had.

From first moving into Earlham, the house teemed with

people. There were the older children; the eldest was nine, then there was Elizabeth aged five and there were four younger ones – all babies really. There were servants, nannies, nursemaids and a governess. Outside there were gardeners, coachmen, grooms and stableboys. In fact it was almost impossible for anyone to be alone if they were seeking peace and privacy. And yet, Betsy felt lonely and afraid. She often cried herself to sleep, so scared was she of the stillness, although in the dead of night there would be babies crying in the night nurseries and nannies and nurse-maids would be bustling about attending to them.

Betsy had just started her school lessons when they moved into Earlham but, being so nervous all the time, she was unable to concentrate on her work. She never learned to spell properly and her grammar was terrible even as a grown woman. Her governess and her brothers and sisters called her stupid and she felt they were right. 'My poor Betsy,' her mother wrote in a letter to a friend, 'I try to help her with her lessons but she is such a fidget and a day-dreamer.'

In a time when women were mostly disregarded as people with any rights of their own, as Quakers believed men and women were equal, all Quaker girls were given as good an education as their brothers. The Gurneys were taught Latin, French, History and Natural History, Music and Art. All this was in addition to the subjects other girls were taught such as sewing, singing, dancing, household economics and how to plan a menu. It was a hard education which began from their earliest days.

Betsy always complained of being ill and no one was ever really sure if she was, or if she just imagined she was ill to get out of lessons. It was fashionable in those days for females to be forever ailing with headaches and fainting fits. It made them appear more feminine and fragile. But the

Gurney girls weren't brought up like that. They were encouraged to be lively and run about in the fresh air with their brothers. They all had ponies and galloped through Earlham Park or rode the three miles into Norwich.

Some days Betsy forgot to be ill and joined in, then suddenly she would claim to feel ill again and become all weak and wilting. Her sisters rather enjoyed her being like that. It was romantic to have a delicate, frail sister who might very soon die – even though they suspected she was as fit as they were. They thought it was only her nervous disposition which made her believe she was ailing. Actually, nervous dispositions were quite stylish as well, so they urged her to lie around looking pale and weak, especially if they had friends visiting the house. All the same *they* didn't want to be fashionable and after gazing at her for a while, off they would scamper with their guests to run through the gardens. They would play by the river or go into the stables or barn where they would hide in the hay or leap from it with their skirts flying around their ears.

Occasionally, Betsy would make a speedy recovery and join in – until she realised she was getting less attention than when she lay pathetically on the sofa. Sometimes she longed to get away from the others to find a bit of peace and quiet. Then when she was alone she was afraid.

One sister, the high-spirited Rachel, had a more gentle nature than the others, and she sympathised a lot with Betsy. As for Betsy, she always felt a bit inferior to her two older sisters, especially to Kate, who was a bit bossy. Still, she and Rachel got on well together and never quarrelled. Whenever Betsy was 'mumping' – the Gurneys' own word for moping – Rachel understood and left her to come round in her own time.

The good relationship between these two gave their mother an idea. She would give them a little room to themselves—one of the old powder closets. It might encourage them to grow even closer, she thought, and Rachel, who was full of life and self-confidence, might pass some of it on to Betsy. They kept all their toys and books in the closet together with Rachel's sea-shell collection. Betsy loved those shells, but she refused to make her own collection because, whenever they were at the seaside, she kept well away from the shoreline where the shells could be found.

The other children resented Betsy being treated like an invalid, and sensing their feelings towards her made Betsy peevish and obstinate. And she was so ashamed of her poor results in the schoolroom and the teasing she had over them that she cried a lot in the little room she shared with Rachel. When she came out for meals, if her eyes were swollen and red, then she said she had poor eyesight. Rachel knew the truth but she never gave her away.

Catherine was the one who most understood her strange little girl. And although she had no favourites amongst her children she tried to keep Betsy close by her. This protected her from all the teasing and, her mother hoped, it would help to overcome her shy nervousness.

Instead it made her worse. Betsy thought her mother was so good and gentle that she feared the Lord might want to take her and keep her with the angels. Then what would become of her? She worried so much about this that she used to pray that the whole family could die at the same time so as never to be apart.

Each morning Catherine visited all her children while they were still in their beds, cots and cradles. After breakfast she would take the little ones for a walk while the older ones got on with their lessons. Unlike most rich ladies, she would even go into the kitchens to see how the servants were getting on and to help the cook to plan the day's menu. Shortly before lunchtime she would go up to the nursery to play with the babies, then in the afternoon she would go to help the older children in the schoolroom.

After the older ones had dined with their parents in the evening, John and Catherine would go up to the night nursery where she would help bathe the babies while their father played with them. Later, Kate, Rachel and Betsy would join their parents for the evening. Then, just before bedtime, they would have a Bible reading and sing a psalm.

It was a happy life for them all, but of all things Betsy liked most to accompany her mother in the garden. They spent hours tending the fruit bushes and flowers. Catherine refused to accept that there were such things as weeds. 'They are all God's plants,' she said. 'The cultivated ones are deliberately planted by people. The rest are wild flowers.'

As a small girl, Betsy really believed she lived in the Garden of Eden, it was so lovely. And when the work was finished she and her mother would sit in the cherry orchard at the back of the house surveying all the wonders of God's plants.

In their happy life, there was one thing the Gurney children hated and that was 'Goats'.

They had a special word, 'dis', for anything they *dis*liked or thought *dis*gusting. And apart from their governess, the most 'dis' thing in the world was 'Goats', their own name for the Goats Lane Meeting House.

Plain Quakers attended Meeting three times a week, but as Wide Quakers, the Gurneys only went once, on Sundays. Still, the children would have avoided even that if they could have. Betsy usually cried or claimed she was too ill to go. This made the others angry as they climbed into the carriage to go. They knew she was being left at home with her grandmother who lived in a wing of their mansion house. And they knew Betsy wouldn't be too ill to eat the little cakes and sugar plums their grandmother would make for her while they were at Goats.

Today Quaker children only attend Meeting for fifteen minutes. When Elizabeth was a child they were expected to stay for the entire Meeting which lasted two hours.

The Meeting House was a long, low, rectangular building. Inside were rows of narrow, wooden benches facing each other. The men and boys, all with their hats on, sat on one side. Women and girls, in their demure linen caps and neckerchiefs, sat opposite. Nearly everyone present was dressed in plain, high necked black or grey clothes. At that time, while most men wore ruffles on their shirts, Quakers considered even buttons and pockets on a garment were a show of vanity.

The Meetings were always open to the public but few non-Quakers wished to attend except occasionally out of curiosity. Very young children would be seated on the front benches where the elders could keep their eyes on them. All the same they got into mischief, pulling faces and giggling at each other. The worst offenders were the Gurneys. They fidgeted, wriggled and uttered loud sighs of boredom that could be heard all over the building.

Although Quakers have no priests or ministers they have the elders. These are people who are treated almost as ministers out of respect for their age or their devotion to the Society of Friends. These unsmiling, stern-faced people would sit on a raised gallery and gaze down on the rest of those gathered below on the benches.

It was the long silences the Gurneys hated most, when everyone waited for the Lord to speak to them through one of the people gathered there. This was usually an elder as they were thought to be better at hearing the Lord speak than most of the others.

As the clock struck ten, the Goats Lane Meeting House doors would be closed and the silence would begin. Sometimes a man or woman would suddenly stand up and repeat what they had heard the Lord saying. At other times a whole two-hour Meeting would pass without anyone feeling God had spoken and the total silence would remain unbroken until twelve o'clock. All the children could do was sit waiting for the clock to chime and it felt more like two days than two hours.

Had the elders and other Plain Quakers used the same word, they would have called the Gurney children 'dis'. There they would be in their vividly coloured clothes of the richest fabrics which rustled as they took their places on the uncomfortable benches. It was bad enough their looking like a row of bright plumaged birds without their bad behaviour. After Meeting, John and Catherine were often 'eldered' over the way their children acted. Being 'eldered' meant having a harsh lecture on their weak, if not actually wicked ways. Richenda always said she would like to get a big stick and hit all the miserable elders on the head with it.

Catherine understood the children's boredom. She had felt the same way when she was little. She tried to explain that, in the long silence, they themselves might hear the Lord speak. The children just grumbled and 'mumped' and their mother worried what would become of them if their thoughts wandered too far from their religious duties.

Betsy wasn't even sure if there was a God, but she didn't dare to say it. As much as she hated going to Goats, she did want to be good and when her mother, who was always working for the poor, went on her charity missions, Betsy loved to go with her.

Although Earlham was in the country, each summer the entire household moved further into the beautiful Norfolk countryside to a smaller house at Bramerton for a holiday.

Close by, in a tiny thatched cottage, lived an old lady who had lost an arm. She couldn't do some of the jobs about the house so Catherine and Betsy went regularly to help her. Then there was Greengrass, an old man who grew delicious strawberries in his cottage garden and gave them all away to his neighbours; this included the Gurneys when they were staying at Bramerton. There was the gardener who attended to the lawns when they'd returned home to Earlham. He was always fishing and taking fish to the Gurneys' cook when they were on holiday.

In return for all these kindnesses, Catherine and Betsy could frequently be seen walking down the leafy lanes to their cottages with covered baskets full of all sorts of delicacies. Betsy never tired of this. They were such happy days that she even forgot to be ill.

When Daniel was born in March, 1791, Betsy was almost eleven. All the children were taken into their mother's room to peep at the new arrival. The older ones led the way, holding the hands of those younger. Joseph, the youngest at two and a half, trotted in holding on to the hem of four-year-old Samuel's frock. In those days little boys wore clothes like their sisters until they were about five.

They all gazed at the tiny baby – something most of them had done lots of times before. This time was different, though. It was to be the last baby born to John and Catherine. But none of them knew that on that happy, spring morning.

3: Growing Up

The year after they moved into Earlham, another baby, Samuel, had been born, and two years later baby Joseph had arrived. Daniel's birth brought the number to eleven and the Gurneys were an extremely happy family for a while.

It was John who first noticed that Catherine was spending a lot of time in her room, resting. At first he thought she was tired with all the responsibility she had: an enormous house and many servants to manage, working for the poor and being an attentive mother to eleven children. But as weeks dragged on it became obvious that she was ill.

Eventually, everyone realised that Catherine was gravely ill. The once noisy household now lived in a hushed atmosphere and a feeling of gloom crept everywhere. The children saw little of their mother. Sometimes they were taken to see her for a few minutes. They would cluster round her bed and whisper their love for her. But Catherine was often too weak to reply to them.

It was a cold, damp autumn. The children had colds and coughs and couldn't play outside. Most of their time was spent in the nurseries in a wing of the house away from Catherine's room so that she wouldn't be disturbed by the sounds of their playing.

Elizabeth was terribly depressed and miserable at her mother's illness. She never joined in their fun and games now because, unlike the other children, even the older ones, Kate and Rachel, she sensed that her mother was going to die.

Catherine knew she was dying and one day, when her dear Betsy crept into her room to pay her a secret visit, the child was upset. Her mother was praying to God to help Kate and to care for the little ones, Samuel, Joseph and Daniel. Betsy ran away heartbroken. She couldn't understand why all the other children had been left out of their mother's prayers, and especially herself. She had always spent so much time in her mother's company, helping her in the garden and visiting the poor.

But Catherine knew that when she died, Kate, the eldest girl, who was still only seventeen, would have to become mother to the whole brood. She also realised it would be harder for the babies to lose their mother than for the older ones, who would be able to understand what had happened to her. The little ones wouldn't understand death and would need all the comfort the Lord could give them.

Days later, on 17th November, Catherine died. From the moment she heard of her mother's death, Betsy went to lie on the mat outside Catherine's bedroom door. Nothing and no one could persuade her to move. She felt she wanted to die too. There was no one to understand her now, not even Rachel, close as the two sisters were.

Kate was marvellous. She immediately took over the running of Earlham. She helped her father to bear his sad loss and she truly did become a mother to all the children — even though they thought she was a bit too bossy. Rachel resented Kate's bustling, busy attitude about the house but she had to admit that Kate was doing a good job.

The housekeeper, Hannah, their old nursemaid, Sarah and John all stood by Kate in her new responsibility, so there was no use the younger Gurneys rebelling against any of their older sister's decisions. Instead, they made every effort to adjust to their new circumstances.

Betsy was the only awkward one.

Although the entire household always got up before six o'clock in the morning, Betsy refused to get up, claiming to have aches and pains. She deliberately missed the lessons she didn't like and she particularly hated French. She wouldn't study at all and this made their 'dis' governess more unpleasant than she normally was. For a punishment, Betsy was made to speak in French to the younger children. If ever she lapsed into English or, to be obstinate, Latin, she was made to pay a fine of one farthing.

After Catherine's death in November, no one at Earlham looked forward to Christmas that year. Unlike the Plain Quakers, the Gurneys had always celebrated in the way non-Quakers did. They had turkey and plum pudding, parties and gifts. The house would be decorated with mistletoe and holly garlands and an enormous yule log would be burning in the grate.

It was because of the nearing festive time that John gathered his inner strength and determined to bring the house back to near normality. He thought it was wrong for young children to live in a house of mourning where the servants went about weeping.

Maybe it was Betsy herself, with her moods, who made up his mind for him. Happiness must be brought back into Earlham. That was surely what his beloved Catherine would have wanted. She wouldn't like her little ones to spend months of their lives in sorrow. She would especially not want twelve-year-old Betsy to fret her own young life away.

Although John himself didn't feel like celebrating Christmas within such a few short weeks of his wife's death, he forced himself to hide his grief for the children's sake.

When Christmas came, there were toys for the little boys

and yards of beautiful silk for dresses for the girls together with books and games for everyone. There was all the usual fare, sweets, mincepies, nuts and all manner of things.

Of course, he was severely eldered by even the Wide Quakers. His brother was very angry. 'Thou hast sinned,' he declared in the quaint way Plain Quakers had of addressing each other as 'thee' and 'thou'.

John didn't try to explain. He knew his brother wouldn't understand his reasons.

Soon after the New Year came in, the weather got worse. That January saw gales and rain. The great house was never really warm and everywhere they looked outside it was grey and depressing. School lessons had begun again after the Christmas break and everyone 'mumped'. Soon the loss of their mother started to show in the children's behaviour. None of them liked their 'dis' governess, and to annoy her they disobeyed her all the time. Kate tried to control them but she was so young and there were too many of them against her.

Their father wasn't much help either. For a long time he had been working at the family bank and was soon to be made a partner in the business. Every day he was out visiting his woollen mill, then going on to the bank. In the evenings and at weekends when he was at home, the children were so pleased to have their only parent all to themselves that he was as boisterous as they were. Often Kate rebuked him as much for his own misbehaviour as for encouraging theirs.

They were becoming so spoiled. In an attempt to keep their minds from their sad loss, nearly every day John brought home expensive toys and new clothes, and generally gave in to their every whim. This helped to keep his own mind off Catherine's death too.

The girls weren't growing up to be prim and ladylike as

young Quaker girls should have been. With their brothers they got up to all sorts of pranks and were rarely chastised for fear of upsetting them. They climbed trees, fell into mud, tore their expensive clothes and played dreadful tricks on visitors.

One day, when their cousin, Hudson Gurney, was visiting them, they locked him in one of the hundred cupboards that Earlham had. When asked by their father where he was, they said, 'We haven't seen or heard of him for a while.' This was true. He'd been locked in the cupboard on one of the top floors of the house for nearly an hour. A search was organised and it was ages before a servant heard the panic-stricken boy hammering on the cupboard door, pleading to be let out.

Betsy was still mourning her mother's death and couldn't bear to see the others laughing and enjoying themselves. She had grown more quiet and withdrawn than ever and her sisters and brothers sometimes forgot she was there. All the same there were odd times when she forgot her unhappiness for a little while. This was usually when there was a trick planned which she simply couldn't resist joining in.

On returning from a business trip to London, amongst other presents, John had brought seven bright red, warmly-lined cloaks for the girls. They tried them on immediately and Samuel, now seven years of age, said they looked like highwaymen. This put an idea in their minds.

The following day, all the girls, except Kate who knew nothing about their plans, walked down the long drive to the main road and waited for the London coach to come along. They all had on their new red cloaks and had taken their brothers along the drive with them. Eventually, from the distance, they heard the sound of horses' hooves.

They all made a human chain across the road and when

the coachman came round a bend in the road and saw them he swiftly reined in his six-horse team and the coach shuddered to a halt. The passengers peered out of the windows and saw a terrifying sight. Even the horses reared up in fright. Whatever was in their path? Were they red-cloaked devils or highwaymen?

After a minute, the children all put out their tongues and ran through the gateway leading to Earlham, all laughing their heads off.

The coachman was furious. He stormed up the Earlham driveway to the door and complained most strongly at what was meant to be a joke. It could have caused an accident with very serious results.

After this, John accepted that his children really were as naughty as people kept telling him they were. He decided that the older boys, John and Samuel, must be sent away to boarding-school where they would learn discipline. The girls were to stay at home and learn the ways of growing into respectable young ladies.

They had grown into beautiful young women but still behaved as children. From then on John saw to it that their lives must be full of the things young ladies normally did. Life became a round of dancing, riding, visiting friends and relations and going on shopping expeditions to Norwich.

Betsy never believed she was as beautiful as her sisters. She did realise, though, at an early age, that she had a very sweet voice. Yet, she could speak with a great authority which usually resulted in her brothers and sisters obeying her wishes without thinking what they were doing.

She not only spoke beautifully. She sang well too, and sometimes in the evening the family would ask her to sing or read aloud to them. These were times when Betsy was happiest because no one was teasing her for her stupidity and lack of learning.

Maybe it was this odd respect the family were beginning to show her that made her feel she wanted to improve herself and do something worthwhile with her life. That would make others respect her too – and not only for her wonderfully musical voice.

She wasn't sure what it was she intended to do – and yet, there was an idea lurking in the back of her mind.

During the years immediately after her mother's death, when the children were left to do as they wished, one of them had one day suggested visiting a 'House of Correction'. This was a sort of prison, and as a form of entertainment anyone could go and pay to see the criminals there. People often visited lunatic asylums too for a day out, or while they were on a picnic.

It doesn't seem possible that they didn't understand what a cruel practice this was. They didn't only go to see the unfortunate inmates of these places. They actually went to make fun of them – especially the poor mad people in the asylums, with their strange antics and wild looks.

Betsy was horrified on her visit but she kept her thoughts to herself for fear of being ridiculed, as she so often was. The sights upset her so much that she had nightmares for a long time afterwards. The memory of that visit kept coming back whenever she thought about what she wanted to do with her future. Somehow, the two belonged together.

Quite suddenly, everyone noticed that Betsy's attitude towards going to Goats had changed. She no longed 'mumped' and complained at it being 'dis'. The elders were pleased to hear of this change. They believed the loss of her mother had caused it, making her want to listen for the voice of God to bring her closer to Catherine.

They were wrong. Betsy liked the long silences because

29

during those spells she was given the opportunity to look within herself and listen for that inner voice we all have.

Something was missing from her life and she was striving to discover what it was. Whenever someone did get up in the Meeting House it was an irritation to her. She didn't want to hear what they had to say or what God was saying through them. She still wasn't sure if there was a God.

No, the silence in the Goats Lane Meeting House was the only peace she knew. Earlham Hall buzzed with noise and activity every day and the silence of the night was no use to her. She was so afraid of the dark that she was too busy listening for creaks and bumps to spend time thinking of her future. All she longed for then was the sweet oblivion of sleep and to awaken in daylight.

With the older boys away at school and their mischief gone with them, the girls settled down a bit. Lessons started at eight o'clock, then they had breakfast. After they'd eaten, Kate gave the little ones a history lesson while the older girls got on with some embroidery. Joseph and Daniel were still with their nurse but they had started to have simple lessons too.

Lunch was at noon, followed by more lessons until three o'clock. They all dined at six o'clock when their father came home, and then, if the weather was fine, they would all go walking in Earlham Park. On autumn evenings when the gardeners were burning rubbish, they would take potatoes from the kitchen and roast them in the bonfire for supper.

They had a riding master and each day they rode their ponies in the parkland or along the avenue of lime trees which made up the long drive leading from the Hall to the road and the outside world. A drawing master from a school in Norwich attended Earlham every week to give art lessons. And, as their governess only had an elementary knowledge of the language, they also had a French master visiting them.

The Gurney children didn't lead the sheltered lives so many of that time did. They knew all that was going on in the world.

On his school holidays, John announced that he no longer took sugar in his tea as a protest against slavery on the West Indies sugar plantations.

At the same time, Betsy was concerning herself with what was going on in France – the revolution. One day she sympathised with the aristocrats. Wasn't she from a high-ranking family? she thought. The French aristocrats couldn't possibly all be evil and selfish any more than all the English ones could be. Yet every day they were being sent to the guillotine. The following day she would change her mind and side with the French peasants and republicans. To prove it, she would even stick the French tricolor in her bonnet.

Her family believed in the movement for universal suffrage (everyone's right to vote), and as Quakers believe men and women are equal, they supported any move to give more rights to women the world over.

Catherine and John had always instilled in their children the idea that people should choose their own way of life, and this included religion, because they had many friends who were not of the Society of Friends. There were Anglicans, Roman Catholics and Unitarians amongst them. People who were no different from Quakers in any way except that they worshipped God in the way they chose.

Of course, for having these views Catherine and John were always being eldered and yet, weren't they simply doing what George Fox had told them to do – allow people to worship in their own way?

31

Some of those they mixed with in fashionable society had begun to scoff at Christianity altogether. The Gurneys decided this had nothing at all to do with them. The people themselves were nice enough.

All the same, when Rachel fell in love with young Henry Enfield, the son of a family friend who was a non-Christian, her father was horrified. He barred Henry from Earlham and forbade Rachel to see him for two years. By then she would be old enough to decide for herself if she wanted to marry a non-believer.

What John didn't realise was that he had a non-believer amongst his own children.

Betsy was confused over her father's decision, especially when he welcomed people of all faiths into his home and didn't even follow his own Quaker faith strictly.

To the Plain Quakers, anyone who didn't believe in the Christian God was wicked and the ugliness inside them showed on their faces. Yet, Betsy could see for herself that some of the most devout Quakers were quite ugly, and they didn't always appear to be the kindest of people either. Hadn't Fox said that pride in physical beauty was wrong? How could a lack of Christian belief show in physical ugliness, then? Some of the non-believers she knew were extremely kind, nice looking and lots more fun than the strict elders.

She was so confused by all this that she was forever lost in deep thought and gloom. Her brothers and sisters tried to avoid her company altogether as she made them feel so miserable. On the warmest, sunniest day, Betsy was like a black rain cloud moving around the house.

They had learned to accept Kate's bossiness as they got older. But if ever Kate was out and Betsy was asked to take over from her, the children hated it. She was far worse than Kate had ever been, ordering them about and being cross all the time.

Her physical health suffered too at this time and her father was so worried that he took her to London to see one of the country's leading doctors.

It was a bitterly cold February morning when they set out for London, and Betsy had a mumping mood. Her sixteenth birthday was a month ahead and she certainly didn't want to be kept away from Earlham for any length of time for any treatment the doctor suggested.

However, when he examined her, he said she was rather a delicate person with a nervous tendency, but there was nothing really wrong with her. She must simply be kept free of all worries and must be sheltered from all unpleasant aspects of life.

The excitement of being in London had a remarkable effect on her, much to her father's surprise. She raced about buying fashionable clothes. She wanted to go to the theatre, to balls and dinner-parties. All the things a young Quaker lady should have turned her back on attracted her like a moth to a flame.

John was delighted to see her so happy – and yet she wasn't happy. At night she felt miserable and guilty for enjoying herself so much through the daytime and evening. After their return to Earlham she fell back into the same miserable Betsy she'd been before they went.

Then, exactly a year later, just before she was seventeen, Prince William Frederick, the nephew of King George III, was invited to Earlham for dinner with the family.

England was under threat of invasion from the French led by Napoleon and all the troops were in readiness to fight for the country. Prince William's troops were barracked at Norwich and John had already met him and liked him.

The house buzzed with preparation. All the girls preened themselves, even Louisa, who was only twelve,

33

because she'd heard the prince was bringing several of his young aides with him.

Uncle Joe Gurney frowned at all the goings-on. He disagreed with the adulation royalty received when everyone was equal in the sight of God. All the same, when his brother invited him and Aunt Jane to come to dinner to meet the prince, he accepted the invitation even though he did insist on addressing the prince as 'thee'. For the grand occasions, musicians were brought to Earlham to play while they dined.

As all the splendid carriages swept up the long drive of budding lime trees, Betsy felt ashamed of herself for the joy she felt surging through her. 'Pomp, pride, vanity, jealousy and ambition are false and empty,' she wrote in her diary later that night when she went to bed. Throughout her life she recorded her guilty feelings in her daily journal as though it were some sort of confessor. If she lost her temper, envied anyone, contradicted or exaggerated and even when she'd mumped, it all went in the diary.

How she enjoyed herself that evening, ignoring the scowling faces of her aunt and uncle, who left as soon as they realised there was to be dancing.

To everyone's astonishment, from the time of the prince's visit, Betsy suddenly brightened up and began to enjoy herself along with the rest of the family – sometimes even more.

'Well, I'm never going to be as good as I should be,' she told Rachel, 'so I may as well be happy with myself the way I am and enjoy myself.'

Prince William Frederick became a close friend of the Gurneys and was always visiting Earlham Hall with his aides. The house rang to the sounds of happy young voices, singing, laughing or just talking.

At night, John would engage a blind fiddler to come and

play while they danced. Sometimes a small orchestra would play in the splendid ballroom that led from the drawing-room.

On other evenings, Betsy and Rachel would play the piano and sing duets. How their audience applauded, but the shy Betsy always felt her beautiful, red-haired sister with her vivid, blue eyes outshone her in everything she did.

On fine days, they would all stroll round the grounds with the prince, visiting the stables or chasing through the shrubberies with the younger children; watching the herons nesting in the park or admiring the peacocks and gazing in wonder at the comings and goings at the dovecotes.

All the time they would be talking about everything they could think of. On the warmest days, the girls would leave their bonnets in the house, let their hair fall loose about their shoulders and pray that Uncle Joe would never hear of such unruly behaviour.

One evening, for fun, the prince suggested Rachel should give a Quaker sermon. For some odd reason, everyone thought the best place for this was in Betsy's bedroom.

Rachel preached like one of the Quaker elders they all knew and hated. How they laughed at the way she mocked the dour old man – but Betsy was uneasy about it.

John was always being eldered by his brother for all the merrymaking at Earlham. He had just been lectured over a wonderful Christmas the family had celebrated two weeks earlier. He was used to that lecture. It had been happening every year from his first marrying Catherine. But when Joseph came to hear of the mock sermon it was the most severe eldering John ever had.

Rachel was included in it and she burst into tears. It wasn't God she'd mocked and ridiculed but the miserable elder. It had been a good and sincere sermon she'd preached.

Uncle Joe would hear none of this and was very harsh with her.

The Gurneys couldn't believe that God didn't have a sense of humour. Surely he laughed and, they suspected, he would be as intolerant of the fault-finding, sour-faced elders as anyone. When Rachel reminded Betsy of this, it eased her conscience a bit. After all, she hadn't preached the sermon – but she had allowed it to be done in her room.

John thought over all his brother had said. Maybe once more he'd let life get out of hand at Earlham. The family were no longer young children. Most of them were young adults. It would do them good to attend Goats a little more often, he decided.

His children were dismayed at this. Only Betsy thought it was right. In a way she was pleased her uncle had stepped in to stop them straying too far from their Quaker duties. Still, she couldn't understand why she should care when she didn't believe in God. And the idea of going to Goats more often filled her with dread.

Those long silences under the stern faces of the elders always ended up with the Gurneys giggling. They just couldn't help themselves and it was almost as if the elders expected them to misbehave – so they did. But, as her father had already been thinking, they were no longer children. It was time they behaved like responsible adults – but could they, Betsy wondered, at Goats?

4: William Savery

In the damp winter of 1798, just before her eighteenth birthday, Elizabeth missed Goats more times than she attended. She was having real coughs, colds and fevers. And she was also going through another spell of confusion in her mind and was very dissatisfied with her life. When all the family were away at Goats, she held her own silences to try to work things out.

While all the singing, laughing and dancing was taking place at Earlham, she was happy. Later, at night, she was full of remorse, remembering the unhappy poor of this world who had nothing to rejoice over.

She wrote in her journal that she thought life was a sort of journey, and 'if I set out along the wrong road, I shall lose my way for ever'.

It was in the February of that winter that William Savery, a well-known Quaker from America, came on a visit to England and would be attending a Friends' Meeting at Goats Lane the following month.

On the Sunday morning of his visit, Goats didn't seem quite so 'dis' to the Gurney brood. Someone from America! That was exciting! They wouldn't have to sit through two silent, boring hours under the sullen elders' gazes, for William Savery would surely feel the urge to speak. What would he say, they wondered? They knew he'd been to most of the countries in Europe. He spoke several languages and, in his own country, he had actually met and preached to Red Indians.

Betsy wasn't as interested as the others but she agreed to go as Uncle Joe had eldered her for missing Goats so often. He accused her of having her old imaginary illnesses again and couldn't accept that she was really ill. His disbelief angered Betsy. And, as she knew her uncle and his elder Friends would be showing much respect and awe for William Savery, she decided to shock them all, including their special guest.

All morning she'd mumped about Goats until finally she came downstairs ready to go. Her father gasped when he saw her. She had chosen the most outrageous clothes to wear. But he was afraid to criticise her for fear of inviting more mumps.

William Savery couldn't believe his eyes when the Gurneys arrived. All the girls were dressed in different hues and resembled a walking rainbow. Their silk petticoats rustled and swished as they moved, and as they took their places he frowned at them – and especially at Betsy.

Under her bright red cloak, she wore a purple dress. Her boots were vivid purple and were tied with scarlet ribbons. On top of her golden ringlets sat an enormous cream poke-bonnet lined with purple silk and tied under her chin with big red ribbons and a bow.

They looked more like a row of gaudy parrots on a perch than a family of Quaker girls, thought Savery.

His scowling reaction delighted Betsy. Her aim to shock was successful. She was a little surprised herself, though, to see a slim, handsome man with black curly hair. He wasn't a young man but all the girls twinkled their eyes at him. This shocked him even more.

There were about two hundred people there that morning. Most of them were wealthy owing to their good reputation for being honest and reliable, qualities which made for success in business. People outside their faith were always puzzled at the way Quakers liked to accumulate lots of money when they believed in the simple life. But to Quakers, money in itself wasn't a bad thing. It could be put to good use for the benefit of others.

All the same, their fellow Quakers disapproved of the way the Gurneys displayed their wealth, and thought it vulgar and alien to their beliefs.

By the time the doors were closed at ten o'clock, the Gurneys were already feeling bored and uncomfortable under the critical elders' gazes. The Meeting House was dreary and colourless. Betsy felt cold and miserable. She wriggled and squirmed about on the hard bench and wished she'd stayed at home. Earlham Hall would be warm, with roaring fires in all the rooms. The chairs were softly cushioned. There were bright curtains, beautiful carpets and splendid ornaments. All the walls were hung with pictures and family portraits. For an instant she thought of her mother's portrait and it saddened her.

She shook the sadness away with a toss of her head and held out her feet in their purple boots to admire the red ties. The other girls giggled, then sighed loudly.

The silence went unbroken for half an hour and even the other young people began to feel restless. Boys and girls started flirting with each other, fluttering eyelashes and casting shy glances across the room.

William Savery was astonished at such behaviour. The elders were used to it and on that morning, they were so embarrassed in the presence of their guest that they pretended not to notice it.

Suddenly, William Savery rose to his feet and stepped out into the little square between the facing benches. He was a tall man and the people were overwhelmed even before he spoke.

The first thing to arrest Betsy's attention was his soft

American accent. It gave his commanding voice a gentleness she wouldn't have suspected from the stern looks he'd been giving her.

For once, all the Gurneys found themselves listening intently to every word. For the first time at Goats they could believe these really were God's words they were hearing through this strangely attractive and gentle man. His frowning countenance had changed to soften his features and he smiled at everyone even as he was speaking.

Betsy knew she would be eldered after the Meeting for dressing the way she was and she drew her colourful boots under her long crinoline dress to hide them from sight. She regretted the way she'd wanted to offend this great man and felt she deserved to be eldered.

The love of God seemed to be pouring out of him, and she began to weep. Her heart filled with remorse for having laughed at religion – often just to appear fashionable. Now, through this man's words, she knew, she simply *knew* there was a God, and his goodness was washing over her. A great choking lump formed in her throat. She fought to control a sob that threatened to escape her as the tears trickled down her face.

How different from all the other mornings at the Goats Lane Meeting House.

When William Savery finished speaking, Betsy still wept. Rachel asked her what was the matter but she couldn't answer.

The Meeting was over. The last hour and a half had sped by without anyone noticing the time and when everyone got to their feet to leave Betsy didn't move.

William Savery was staying at their Uncle Joe's house, the Grove, and a few days before the Meeting, their uncle and Aunt Jane had invited John, his children and some of the elders to have lunch with them.

The young Gurneys protested. Goats in the morning and again in the evening was bad enough. Expecting them to go to the Grove afterwards to have lunch with the elders was asking too much.

Their father agreed. If he forced them to go he might only regret it afterwards if they misbehaved.

To everyone's surprise, instead of making for the Meeting House door, Betsy walked over to where the men and boys sat and begged her uncle to forgive her for refusing his invitation. She would love to have lunch with him, Aunt Jane, William Savery and the elders.

John was astonished at this change in his most troublesome daughter, but he was pleased – even if she was dressed badly for the occasion.

Although she was the niece of the host, Betsy felt like an intruder at the table. She was the only Wide Quaker there except for her father, who was dressed soberly in comparison to her.

William Savery was indeed a great man, and Betsy thought he was more of a real Quaker than all the others present, including Uncle Joe and Aunt Jane. She'd always thought that about her own parents, though. They were sincere in their faith without being over-pious and glum about it. William Savery smiled a lot, and there was a goodness and warmth even in his smile.

He was talking about his travels and about his meetings with the Red Indians. Betsy was very impressed by his attitude towards these 'heathens' when he said he liked and pitied them.

Uncle Joe and his guests were obviously disturbed at this and shifted uncomfortably in their chairs. Betsy could almost feel their indignation oozing out of them at such a statement. Still, they respected their honoured guest too much to challenge him, so they sat listening,

E.F.—3

and eventually they began to understand what he meant.

Heathens weren't wicked. They were deprived unfortunates not to know the love of God. There were even people in England who didn't believe in the Christian God and they too were to be pitied, not scorned. Who scorns a baby for being helpless? Do we leave it to starve because it cannot feed itself? Do we mock it when it cannot talk or walk? No. We teach it. We teach it what we are fortunate to know ourselves.

Savery went on to say that he hadn't gone amongst the Red Indians to preach the word of God. First he learned their language and their ways and then he went to talk to them of their ways and of their gods. Only then did he speak of his own Christian God. The Indians were curious to know more. And the more he told, the more they liked this great God and wanted to know him for themselves.

It took a while for the narrow-minded Quakers to understand him. They lived in such a small, close community, knowing little of the outside world. This was common for people at that time. They didn't travel as freely or as widely as we do today. There was no television or radio. And to some, even books and newspapers were useless as not many could read.

That evening, Betsy was actually impatient to return to Goats at six o'clock for the evening Meeting. Her Uncle Joe was so pleased to see his niece enthralled by his guest that he'd asked if she would like to travel to Goats Lane alone in the coach with William Savery.

She was overjoyed, and on the journey it was as if the two were holding a private Friends' Meeting.

She'd wanted to change into a more suitable dress for her next Meeting with the great man but decided against it. Everyone was used to the Gurneys' flamboyant clothes. To appear suddenly at the evening Meeting in a simple dress

42

would draw more attention to herself than if she kept the same one on. They might even suspect her of mocking them.

True Quakers didn't attract attention to themselves, nor would she in future. Something had happened to her within a few hours. It was as if she was a different person from when she awoke that morning. Betsy wondered if she had only started to awake at the morning Meeting when she discovered finally that there was a God.

While travelling to Goats Lane she told William Savery how she felt. When she mentioned her dress he patted her hand and smiled understandingly.

Napoleon seemed intent on conquering the whole world. Some of the younger Quaker men had felt unable to accept their pacifist roles. They had renounced their faith and joined the army to fight for peace. Others, following their true faith, volunteered to go to the battlefields of Europe to tend the fallen – even giving succour to their wounded and dying enemies. At the second Meeting that day, William Savery spoke out against the evils and horrors of war and prayed for the safe and speedy return of all those who had become involved.

After the Meeting, John asked the Friends' guest if he would have breakfast with his family at Earlham the following morning, and he accepted.

There was no difficulty in getting Betsy out of bed that day. How everyone gaped when she entered the breakfast-room. That morning, in the privacy of her own home and family, for the first time, Betsy rejected all her finery and wore a plain, dark green gown with a white silk neckerchief and white cap. At the family's reaction, the shy girl flushed as bright red as the cloak she'd worn at Goats – and would never wear again.

William Savery appreciated her effort and knew what it must have cost when he saw her embarrassment. Only the night before she'd told of how her sisters and brothers always teased her and thought her peculiar. He had children of his own and his heart went out to her. Once she was seated at the table, she was too interested in all he had to say to notice the odd glances everyone was giving her. She even forgot to eat her breakfast.

A few days after William Savery left Norwich to continue his travels, Betsy went into the city to do some shopping. When she began receiving admiring glances from the people she passed—some of them Prince William Frederick's officers—she was amazed. For a moment she felt a surge of pride, then a guilty flush crept over her for being vain. Although she was very graceful and beautiful, it never occurred to her that she was. Her sisters were far prettier, she thought, and she had never been the object of so much attention before from strangers.

Betsy didn't realise it was her moods and her shyness that made people sometimes avoid her. That day there was something different about her. A glow of self-confidence radiated from her. She sat straight in the saddle with her head held high instead of slumping with downcast eyes. No one that day could fail to notice the lovely, fair-haired girl riding through the city streets. They didn't know she had found God and through him had discovered her real self.

John saw there was some change in Betsy but he didn't know what it was. After some days, she found the courage to tell him exactly what had happened to her. Her sisters suspected why she wanted to speak to her father and thought she was 'dis'.

Alone in the study, father and daughter faced each other for a full minute before she spoke. And John wasn't prepared for what he was about to hear.

'Father,' she said, 'I've made up my mind, from now on, I shall be a Plain Quaker.'

'A Plain Quaker!' gasped John. 'Oh, my dear. I know what a good influence our dear Friend William Savery had on you—and on us all. But there's no need to go to such lengths to prove it.'

Betsy was furious. She had chosen to change her ways. She hadn't been forced into it and her mind was fully made up.

After their discussion John spent sleepless nights thinking over what had been said. Betsy was well known for her impulses. He remembered when she was fourteen at the time of the French Revolution. She could never decide from one day to the next which side to support. But that was in the past, when she was a child and everyone could smile at her passing moods.

At eighteen, suddenly to want to adopt the severe ways of their faith—ways that her own family refused to follow. This must be the worst impulse she had ever had. What if she changed her mind later? John groaned when he thought of the scorn she would bring down on her own head from the other Plain Quakers and especially from the elders.

Some days later they had another discussion. John didn't say outright that he thought she was being impetuous. He remembered her anger of a few days earlier. With tact he advised her to think hard about her decision. He suggested she go to London and spend some time there. He knew this would be a great test of her new faith. If it could stand up to the gay social life of London, then it wasn't just a whim.

After her two years' separation from Henry Enfield, Rachel had decided not to marry him but to keep to her Quaker beliefs. If she married a non-Quaker—marrying 'out' as it was called—she would be expelled from the Society of Friends, and her faith had proved stronger than the love she thought she had for Henry.

Now John was to put Elizabeth to the same test, though in complete contrast from that of Rachel. He travelled with his daughter in their sumptuous coach and left her in the care of some relatives.

Her days were spent riding in the London parks, visiting art galleries and museums and shopping for stylish clothes. In the evenings she would attend grand balls or the opera and on one occasion she went to the theatre to see *Hamlet*.

For these outings she had her soft flaxen hair done up in curls on top of her head to look elegant. On other occasions it would be parted down the centre from her forehead right down the back of her head where it was caught up in a knot to make her look demure. Her favourite new evening dress was of white silk. It had a blue satin sash and the skirt floated as she walked. She even wore face powder.

Her stay in London lasted eleven months, far longer than she'd intended, and she arrived home on the 16th April, a month before her nineteenth birthday. She looked so well and was laden down with gifts for everyone.

John was delighted to have her home but he was pleased he'd persuaded her to give her idea a trial. It was clear that it had been an impulse all the time. How surprised he was when Elizabeth announced she felt even stronger about becoming a Plain Quaker. If her father had been testing her faith then so had she.

All the glittering balls and theatres, all the lovely clothes were unable to turn her away from her decision. It was a severe test which resulted in her certainty that her chosen path was the right one.

Almost a year's absence from Earlham helped others to accept this change in Betsy Gurney rather than if she'd made a sudden change in a matter of days. She was still a little too shy to wear the really Plain Quaker dresses of grey or black. They would only make her stand out from her sisters in their bright colours – the very opposite from what she wanted to do. Instead, she settled for subdued colours of dark blue, wine red and her favourite dark green but all without adornment apart from a watch hung on a gold chain about her neck. Her scarlet cloak and feathered hats were put away, to be replaced by cloaks matching the colours of her dresses. And she wore the simple little white caps of cotton or organza that all Quaker women were expected to wear.

Throughout her life, though, she never could bring herself to use the Plain Quaker way of addressing people as 'thee' or 'thou'. She always though it sounded affected and insincere.

Betsy was a happier person once she'd found 'the right road', the phrase she had used in her journal a year earlier. Yet, if she was happier, she still wasn't content. She desperately wanted to help people less fortunate than herself. But at nineteen she was really too young to get involved with anything of great importance and be taken seriously. With her wealth she could give away money. But the Gurneys were always doing that anyway and it didn't satisfy her longing to do something worthwhile.

William Savery wrote often to her after he was back in America. In answering his letters, Betsy told him how she hoped to hear the Lord tell her what she must do. But at every Friends' Meeting, throughout the long silence, she heard nothing.

William Savery explained that 'she was not yet on the right road'. Betsy was merely at the crossroads. He told her to be patient and the right road would be pointed out to her. Maybe the Lord himself hadn't reached a decision for her.

Life at Earlham Hall went on as normal. Betsy didn't frown on the merrymaking of the others as they'd expected her to. She sometimes felt tempted to join in, especially with the dancing she loved so much. There were even times when she felt little pangs of envy at the sight of her sisters in lovely gowns and jewels.

Neither the great house nor the nearby River Wensum were frightening to her now. She felt God walked with her wherever she went. There was nothing to fear, not even in the darkest night. Instead of lying listening for spooky sounds, she was free to think of the future ahead of her. What was it to be? Which path would the Lord direct her along? she wondered.

Weeks went by but no sound came through the silences, nor did she hear him in the stillness of the night.

Then one day she heard about the sick wife of one of the prince's young soldiers. She was a delicate creature who was expecting her first baby. Some days she was too weak to get out of bed to cook or clean the house. Betsy remembered the holidays at Bramerton during her childhood and of how she would go with her mother to help the neighbours.

She immediately put on her riding-habit and went into Norwich. But it was a completely different Betsy from the one who'd flirted with the young officers as she passed by in earlier years.

She went directly to the soldier's house where she found the young wife struggling to get up from her sick bed. Betsy made her stay where she was while she set to, doing some cleaning jobs around the house. She had also taken a basket of delicious food which would last the couple for some days.

On the way home, she began to wonder if this was the sign she'd been waiting for. Helping the woman made her feel good inside – so good that it bordered on pride, and that was something she was determined to resist.

Elizabeth wasn't perfect and she was the first to admit it. Once, in her journal, she had written, 'I must not flirt. I must not be bad-tempered with the children. I must not exaggerate. I am more cross, more proud, more vain, more extravagant. If only I had a little religion.' Well, now she had her religion, but all the same she realised she was still a human being with many flaws.

The first inkling of where her destiny really lay was one sunny day when she went out alone for a walk in the lanes around Earlham Hall and nearly stumbled over a little boy. He was very dirty and both he and his ragged clothes smelled dreadfully. But he had a pleasant face and he smiled sheepishly when she looked him up and down and asked, 'What is your name?'

5: A New Life and Joseph Fry

'Billy,' the child mumbled, and stood there while she asked more questions. He didn't know how old he was nor when it was his birthday. He didn't know what a school was. He couldn't read, write or count.

Betsy was filled with pity and decided there and then, 'I'll teach him.'

'Come with me,' she said in her sweet yet commanding voice. The child put his grubby, thin little hand in hers and allowed himself to be taken along to Earlham, the sight of which terrified him.

On the way Betsy began to worry. This was her first encounter with the 'poor'. Sometimes in London, or even in Norwich, she'd seen and heard dirty, rough people fighting, swearing and staggering about in drunkenness. They attacked people and smashed property. Would she regret taking Billy into her home? she wondered. One look at his frail, bony frame assured her that it was safe. A good meal would hardly give him enough energy to behave like a vandal.

It didn't occur to her that Billy was afraid of this beautiful fine lady, the likes of whom he'd never seen before. When he saw the mansion and she said he was going inside, his body began to quake. What was she planning to do with him? Only his manly pride prevented him from showing fear.

Betsy had another worry. What would the family say

when she arrived home with this half-starved, grubby mite?

Her worry was needless. For one thing, they were always prepared for anything Betsy did. For another, as Quakers, they were happy to receive the poor child into their home.

After he'd been taken to the kitchen and been fed by their bewildered cook, Betsy took him upstairs to the magnificent drawing-room to read him a story from the Bible. At first, Billy gaped at all the splendour surrounding him. Then when she began the story, he was enthralled by her words.

An hour later she took him to the door, said 'Goodbye' and asked if he would like to come again the following day for another story. This was the way William Savery would work, she thought. If Billy hears enough stories, then, like the Red Indians, he will be curious and want to read for himself. That would be the time to teach him. Not only would he learn to read and write. With stories from the Bible, he would learn of God.

Betsy was more successful than she imagined. The next day, Billy brought his brothers and sisters. Two days later, he arrived with a bunch of friends and cousins.

The orderly way of Earlham was in a shambles. The servants were angry at all the dirt the children brought into the house on their feet. After a week of the schooling, with their dirty clothes, the silk-covered chairs and couches were looking grimy too.

The family were very annoyed. Betsy was being so unfair, putting the servants to so much extra work, cleaning carpets and furniture as well as washing the covers and the floors. She also expected cook to provide food for far more mouths than she had catered for.

Someone reminded her that the servants were not her slaves. Betsy was so upset when her thoughtlessness was pointed out that she lay awake all night trying to overcome the problem. Finally she found the answer. In the Earlham grounds were many outhouses, and they weren't all in use. One of them could be turned into a schoolroom.

When the local people heard of Miss Elizabeth Gurney's school, they wanted to send their children too. Soon they were coming from the surrounding farms and cottages until there were a hundred children gathering at Earlham every day.

Soon the household settled back to normal and the irate servants had calmed down again. Then the family and staff agreed that it was a good idea for Betsy to set up her school. During class time, her sisters would go and listen at the door. Passing servants would stop a while and peek in at the window.

Because they lived in the country, those children were amongst the luckiest of England's poor at that time. The needy town children were put out to earn their living at such an early age that they weren't much more than babies. They might have been born in the country but their parents would have moved to the towns and cities. There they could find work down the mines or in the new factories and mills that were being built up and down the land.

Seven-year-olds were up before the crack of dawn to make their way to their place of employment. By the time they returned in the evening it was dark, and some never saw daylight. When a famous doctor was asked, 'Is it right for these children to work twenty-three hours a day?' he replied, 'They may not be able to work twenty-four.'

Mine work was the worst of all because the children were treated like beasts of burden. Harnessed to tubs full of newly hewn coal, they were made to drag them to the bottom of the pit shaft where the coal could be hauled to the surface.

To see the fortunate ones in her charge looking happy and knowing they were being educated, reflected on Betsy. She glowed with an inner happiness, although she still had bouts of illness. But now, when she was feeling unwell, the family sympathised and gave her more attention than when she was young and always complaining.

Later that year, when the young Gurney boys came home from boarding-school for their holidays, Betsy gave her pupils a holiday too. John was taking his family to Wales to visit their cousin Priscilla. It wasn't their first visit to her but it was the first Betsy had ever really looked forward to, sad as she was at leaving her pupils.

Priscilla, or Cilla as she was called, belonged to Bath. Her family still lived there and enjoyed the revelry and sparkle of that smart and genteel city. But Cilla had turned her back on it all to become a Plain Quaker.

The journey from Earlham took several days. At nights they stayed in inns along the way. The weather wasn't too good for the time of year and was often cold and wet. The family would huddle together in the evenings around the blazing fires, chatting while the innkeeper would bring them hot drinks and plates of toasted muffins. It was a lovely, carefree time. And yet, Betsy sensed something of great importance to her future was going to come of this holiday – and she was right.

One afternoon, while Betsy's brothers and sisters attended a concert with their father, Cilla took Betsy to visit a friend of hers, Deborah Derby, another Plain Quaker.

At Deborah's house there were more guests, and one, Rebecca Young, took a liking to Betsy and watched her throughout the afternoon.

After tea they held a silence, and soon Deborah quietly rose to her feet. Without looking at Betsy, she began to speak, telling of what God had said during the silence.

Betsy felt the same awe as when she had first heard William Savery. Deborah seemed to be talking straight to her, as though trying to pass on a message.

When she'd finished speaking, Rebecca Young stood up. Unlike Deborah, she deliberately faced Betsy and said that the Lord had told her, 'I want thee, Elizabeth Gurney, to be a Light to the blind; Speech to the dumb and Feet to the lame.'

Betsy felt prickles and shivers running from her neck and down her back. Tears welled up in her eyes and a great humility swept over her. There was no mistaking what they were telling her, was there? God was wanting her to be a minister. Not an ordained minister, Quakers don't have them, but one of the elders who were more likely to hear God speaking than others.

In her journal that night she wrote, 'Can this be? Can I ever be one? If I am obedient, I believe I shall.'

There had never been a time when she'd felt the urge to speak at a Meeting but now she was sure that some day she would. But when would it be?

Shortly after the holiday ended and they were back at Earlham another great change came into Betsy's life in the shape of Joseph Fry.

Like herself he was tall but not very slim. He had dark hair, a wide mouth and eyes that were rather small. He was more pleasant-looking than handsome. Betsy had met him before, when she was staying in London, but it had been only a brief introduction.

Unknown to her, Joseph had found her very attractive on that one meeting. Like her father he was a wealthy banker, and made business an excuse to travel to Earlham to see Betsy again. He stayed for a few days and the two spent so much time together that, by the end of the week, Betsy suspected she was falling in love with him.

After his return to London he wrote frequently and made

many visits to Norwich even though it was such a long, tedious journey. All the Gurneys could see how fond they were of each other, and, on one of Joseph's visits, no one was surprised when he asked Betsy to marry him.

Much as she wanted to marry him, this gave Betsy a lot of concern. If she married Joseph how could she devote her life to God and become a minister?

Although Quakers believed men and women were equal, the elders would never approve of a wife neglecting her husband and home. She could do charitable work but not to the extent she believed the Lord had planned for her. Hadn't he, through Deborah Derby and Rebecca Young, instructed her to do it? Taking care of a husband, a home and someday maybe children, would be a full-time occupation. A minister would be expected to travel, to give talks as William Savery had done on his tour of Europe.

In a long and sleepless night she went over and over in her mind what she should do. In the end she reasoned that it was God who was directing her to marriage with this good and dear man.

The following morning at Meeting she had doubts about her decision. Perhaps during the silence she would hear God telling her what she must do. But no sign came. It was another elder who spoke that morning, and through him came the message for Betsy. The ministry was not for her – not yet. One day it would be but in the meantime her duty lay in another direction.

In a way she was relieved. Not yet twenty, the very idea was frightening. The Society of Friends showed great respect for the reformed daughter of John Gurney but would they accept her as a minister?

She cast a glance about her. Even as a Plain Quaker she still stood out from the others – more so now. She didn't dress like her sisters, nor did she dress like the rest of them at the Meeting. She looked years younger than her age and the plainness of her clothes only emphasised her beauty and the fairness of her golden hair. It would have been difficult to convince the elders she was someone to listen to.

Betsy didn't know it would be a further nine years before she spoke at a Meeting.

On a warm, sunny Sunday in August that year, 1800, Betsy Gurney became Mrs Elizabeth Fry.

The Goats Lane Meeting House was packed with people to witness the occasion. It was a very simple ceremony. No one married them. A Quaker couple just stand up in front of all those gathered for the occasion and declare their love and respect for each other. Then they go on to say they wish to be married and live together for ever. From then on they are man and wife.

The style that year was frilled, brilliantly coloured floral gowns with low necklines and lots of ribbons and lace, and all her sisters were dressed like that. Elizabeth wore a silk wedding gown and bonnet with no lace or ribbons.

All Joseph's strict Quaker relatives were there and they looked very forbidding. Elizabeth was a bit scared of them, and she was sad too. The rest of her life would be spent in London in their company, far away from her beautiful Norfolk and the happy atmosphere of Earlham Hall. Tears brimmed in her eyes, and her father wept too. He was losing the first of his daughters in marriage. But he knew Joseph loved her very much and he prayed she would settle down to be a good wife.

The day before the wedding had been sad for her when she called her pupils together and said goodbye. The children cried and so did she, but there was no other way. Betsy Gurney was destined for a new life.

Although the Frys were very rich, Joseph himself didn't have as much money as the rest of his family. The house they went to live in, Mildreds Court, in London, actually belonged to some of his relatives. This made them feel that all the family and their friends had the right to visit the house at any time and stay as long as they liked.

To Elizabeth's annoyance the house was always full, and sometimes their visitors were strangers. The Quarterly Meetings were held there too. These were times when elders from all over the country travelled to meet each other to bring their records and reports up to date concerning births, marriages and deaths.

Elizabeth was unable to protest against this as it wasn't her home. And it was very hard for a young wife suddenly to be put in such a situation. Her sister Kate had had a lot of experience of household management ever since the time of their mother's death. Elizabeth had none.

Their first child was a girl, born a year after they married and called Catherine after Elizabeth's eldest sister, who always got called Kate anyway.

Two years later came Rachel, then John the year after, William in 1806, Richenda in 1808 and Joseph in 1809. With all the children bearing the same names as her own brothers and sisters Elizabeth remembered the fun they'd had at Earlham Hall when she was a child. Joseph's family would never approve of such goings-on at Mildreds Court.

The visitors continued to arrive and Elizabeth wished she could just be left alone in peace with Joseph and their own little family. But she remembered her wifely duties and didn't complain.

Shortly before Joseph was born in 1809, his mother felt her old longings beginning to stir. She told herself it was nonsense but she still wanted to take the ministry. To keep her mind from it she began to teach the servants how to read and write. She held silences with them too but she never got up to speak.

Then one afternoon the house was, as usual, full of people. They were still sitting at the tea-table when, instead of wishing they would all go home, as she often did, Elizabeth had a surge of love pass through her – not just for those present but for everyone in the world.

She was sure God was amongst them. And it took a lot of control to stop her from getting to her feet to speak, although there was no silence being held. Almost immediately, one of the guests stood up and began to speak, saying everything that had been passing through Elizabeth's mind. So the Lord had finally let her hear him.

Later that year, in the autumn, the Gurney family sent for her to go to Norfolk as her father was ill. Elizabeth hastily made arrangements and left the following morning.

She was heartbroken when she arrived at Earlham to see how ill he was. There was no doubt in her mind that he was dying. It was only a matter of weeks since he'd visited her in London and now, here he lay, weak and pale. That evening she wouldn't leave his bedside and it was late at night when she was persuaded to go to her bed and sleep. It was a long, weary journey from London and no one wanted her to become ill as well as her father.

The following morning she was up early. But before she could reach her father's room, he died peacefully in his sleep. She tried to run along the landing to his bedroom but her legs were like lead and she was bowed down with grief. Eventually she forced herself to go in, and instantly all her sorrow left her. A glow of happiness swept over her and she dropped to her knees to pray.

Those in the room were astonished until she explained her joy. John had been a good and happy man. Everyone liked him. He'd known little suffering in his life except on the death of his wife. But Catherine had left him the love of all his children.

What Elizabeth didn't realise was that she hadn't prayed silently. She had spoken.

At John's funeral her Uncle Joe spoke at the graveside. Then, just as the family were moving away, without feeling anything, Betsy suddenly sank to her knees and began to speak the same words she'd said on the morning of his death.

The family were embarrassed at the attention she was drawing to herself outside, in public, on her knees. But she saw no one. It was minutes before she let herself be led away from the grave. Like all Quaker graves, it was unmarked and unadorned.

Only weeks later, Joseph Fry's own father died. So soon after her own father's death, Elizabeth was able to give him much comfort. Through her, Joseph too was able to feel gratitude for the good life his father had known. Elizabeth felt different after these two people were gone from their lives. She was only twenty-nine, yet it was as if she became much older in a matter of weeks.

On his father's death, Joseph inherited the Fry family home where he had lived as a child, Plashet House in Essex. It was lovely to be living in the country again, away from the city with its smoke and buildings all around her.

Plashet House was much bigger than Mildreds Court and the family could spread out more into its many, good-sized rooms. There was another advantage too: they owned this house. No one could move in if and when they wanted. In future, it would only be at the invitation of Elizabeth and Joseph.

Now she had more time to do the things she wanted rather than forever be entertaining guests, so she opened another little school. Her scholars were so poor that she decided to feed their bodies as well as their minds. But remembering all the trouble she'd given the servants at Earlham, Elizabeth opened a soup kitchen.

59

This is a place where poor people, without money to buy food, can go each day to be given a meal, usually a bowl of hot soup and a chunk of bread. It may not seem much today. But to people – even small children – who went for days without a bite to eat, it must have been like a feast.

When a group of gypsies moved into some nearby derelict cottages, Elizabeth went to visit them. She asked if there was anything they needed or anything she could do for them. Because she was a Quaker and they were Irish, she thought they might think she was interfering. Wisely, she asked the priest from the local Roman Catholic church to go with her.

These two became firm friends and helped each other in their work. The strict Quakers were suspicious of this, but Elizabeth smiled. It was only what her parents would have done. Still, they weren't Plain Quakers. She was. The gypsies grew to love Elizabeth and soon their children were going to her school.

In 1811, when Joseph, the youngest child, was two, there was another baby. Joseph wanted her to be called Elizabeth after her mother. But her mother wondered if it was a wise name to choose. After all, she had always been the odd one out in the Gurney family. Fortunately neither parent could know that this child was to cause far more heartache than her mother ever did.

6: Newgate Prison

Plashet House, their new home in Essex, was about six miles from London and the Frys were able to visit the city frequently.

On one of these trips, while having supper with some friends, they met some other Quakers who had just been to visit Newgate Prison. Newgate was a most terrible place. Today, the Old Bailey Law Courts stand on the spot where it used to be. But until it was demolished, justice seemed to be the last thing you could expect to find there.

The visitors were so distressed at what they had seen that they felt sick and couldn't eat. Mindful of the effect their account would have, they waited until everyone else had finished their supper before they spoke about it.

They told of iron railings behind which the prisoners could be observed like creatures in a zoo. In fact, the prisoners themselves were so wild and savage that it took a double row of railings to contain them. They were half-naked and freezing cold. Some were fettered, others manacled with heavy chains. And the poor wretches who weren't fighting and clawing at each other held out their filthy and torn hands to the sightseers, screaming for food. Most of their viewers jeered and laughed at them.

At this horrific account, shivers ran through the company. Something must be done to stop such awful suffering. All agreed on that.

But what? After all, they were convicted criminals.

But crime then was completely different from what we consider as crime today.

For the silliest of reasons, nearly all of us would have had relatives in prison at some time in the past. One of Elizabeth's ancestors spent time there. In their days of persecution, at one stage, all the Meeting Houses were closed to prevent the Quakers from getting in. In defiance, the braver ones held Meetings outside. In the seventeenth century, five hundred Quakers died in prison for holding Meetings in Friends' homes or farm buildings.

By the nineteenth century, little had changed. Those imprisoned in Newgate – or any other prison – weren't all bad people. In many cases, they were simply poor. Quite often the most wicked of all were those in charge of them: the warders, or turnkeys as they were then called.

Gaolers needed no qualifications or training of any kind. And it was usually only the lowest types of people who did the job. Not even prison governors treated their prisoners as anything better than animals.

Some of the guests at the supper party thought the dreadful stories were exaggerated. Not Elizabeth. She remembered her childhood visit to the House of Correction and determined to go and see for herself.

Anyone could get into prison. They were like the old Roman arenas where spectators paid to be entertained by watching the sufferings of others.

Remember, early last century was an age when the most common entertainments were bull, bear and dog baiting. Cock-fighting was another popular sport. For this, spikes were fastened to the birds' legs, then they were let loose to tear each other to shreds.

But of course, at that time, people enjoyed public executions.

Close to Elizabeth's old family home stood Norwich

Castle, the great Norman fort built in 1220. It was a prison for centuries. And until just over one hundred years ago, hangings took place right outside the gates. Crowds came to watch and food and drink would be sold to make the event into a picnic.

Elizabeth was always sickened at the thought of such things. She wondered how anyone could be so insensitive. And she knew her visit to Newgate was going to be a horrific experience for someone of her delicate nature. The very next day, she went to the prison. But once inside it wasn't really what she expected. It was far worse.

The turnkeys were drunken, ignorant louts. The place really was freezing. The prisoners were starving, half-dressed and near to madness in their misery.

She was expecting another baby at that time and the smell of the prisoners and their surroundings made her feel sick, so sick that she could only stay for a few minutes. When she got home, she could hardly bring herself to tell Joseph of the sights, even less of the pitiful moaning, howling and screaming made by the wretched inmates. He fussed around her and said she shouldn't have gone when her health wasn't too good.

Elizabeth didn't regret going. By now she was a recognised minister in the Society of Friends and often spoke at Meetings. But the elders made exception for her. With her large family and home to see to, besides running her school and helping the poor, she wasn't expected to travel to distant Meeting Houses as ministers normally were. They would have been astonished had they known what was in her mind that night. After her baby was born and weaned, she intended making regular visits to Newgate.

It was not to be. After Hannah was born, her mother wasn't well for a long time. And all the work she was already involved in took much of her strength.

When Hannah was two, Louisa was born and Elizabeth was forced to admit that a mother of nine children would never have the time to work for the prisoners in Newgate – and she wept for them.

But a year after Louisa was born, little Elizabeth, who was then four, suddenly fell ill and within days she died. Her parents were heartbroken. Elizabeth remembered her doubts over giving the child her own name and she blamed herself for her death.

Joseph recovered from the tragedy more quickly than his wife. For a long time she was unable to think clearly about anything. A year later there was another baby, Samuel. Still, even his arrival did nothing to ease her sorrow at losing little Elizabeth.

Because of the severe winter, they'd moved into their old home, Mildreds Court, for a few months. It was more convenient for Joseph than having to travel to his London bank each day from Plashet House, especially when the roads were under snow.

The house was full of guests just then as it was time for the Quarterly Meeting. Joseph couldn't bear to see his wife so unhappy, so, one evening, to try to keep her mind from her grief, he began to talk about Newgate. Could he renew her interest in the work she'd set her heart on three years earlier? he wondered.

When the strict elders in the house heard of this they couldn't understand him – a man encouraging his wife to take on such a task. Her duty lay in the home and here he was, urging her to neglect it.

But Joseph was concerned for her health. If Elizabeth didn't soon improve, she might pine to death.

After a lot of persuasion, she could see he was right. Her fretting was causing her to neglect her family and domestic duties anyway. She must come back to reality, and nothing would spring a person back to reality faster than a visit to Newgate.

The January morning was bitterly cold when Elizabeth arrived at the prison. Wisely she was wrapped in her ermine-lined cloak and matching muff. When she asked the governor to admit her to the inner part of the women's section his mouth fell open in bewilderment.

'Oh, no, my dear Mrs Fry,' he said, 'you will be able to view the prisoners just as well from this side of the railings.'

Elizabeth drew herself to her full height and looked directly into his cold eyes. In her sweet, yet compelling voice she repeated her request. 'I have no wish to view them. I am here to visit them. To talk and ask if there is anything I can do to improve their appalling conditions.'

The man was speechless. He was also unable to refuse her.

It is fortunate for the world that Elizabeth belonged to two powerful and influential families. Anyone from the lower ranks of society would never have dared to say such a thing. She would have been seen as a trouble-maker and been thrown out, or she could well have ended up in prison herself. As she was the daughter of John Gurney from Norwich and the wife of Joseph Fry, the governor could only humbly grant her permission to enter the place where he would never dare to set foot alone for fear of being ripped to pieces.

Knowing it would be unkind to appear before them so warmly clothed, she left her cloak and muff in the governor's office. How she shook with nerves and cold as she went out into the passage and walked to where two turnkeys were on duty.

They were dirty, whiskery, ignorant men. Unlike the governor they'd never heard of the Gurney or Fry families. When Elizabeth asked to be admitted to where the women were screaming and fighting, they laughed at her and called her a 'silly woman'.

A silly woman! No man had ever spoken to her like that. Quakers treated all men and women with respect. Angrily she glared at them and demanded to be let in.

'Go 'ome and do some embroidery,' one said.

But when Elizabeth showed them the permit from the governor they stopped arguing.

'You won't come out of there alive,' one scoffed.

The other said, 'Better leave me that watch and chain. They'll tear it off your neck . . . and the fancy clothes off your back.'

Her clothes were anything but fancy. As for her watch, she decided it would be as safe on the inside of the gate as in the turnkey's hands.

In that instant, no one would have dreamed this was once the little girl who was 'afraid of her own shadow'. And the doctor who told her father she must be kept from all the unpleasant aspects of life? He would never have recognised her in this erect, self-assured woman.

The massive metal gate was unlocked and with a loud scraping and clanking was pulled back for her to pass through. The howling mob on the inside stopped fighting. All the terrifying sounds faded to silence as she stood there, towering over the cowed wretches.

Outwardly she showed no fear. Inside she trembled. Were the turnkeys right? Would she be attacked? she wondered.

From out of the crowd, a small, scrawny child tottered over on his frail legs and gazed in wonder at the beautiful lady standing before him. She smiled down at him and had a fleeting memory of Billy. She thought too of her own plump, healthy, happy children at home with their nannies and nursemaids. In the next instant she stooped, tickled him under his chin and said, 'Hello'.

He smiled at her and all the women drew nearer, filled with curiosity.

Elizabeth was revolted by the smell of the child and the group of prisoners advancing on her. But being sensitive to their feelings, she stopped herself from wrinkling her nose. Instead she smiled and said, 'Hello. May I stay and talk to you for a while?'

No one in prison ever spoke to them like that. Some had never heard such politeness in all their lives.

The two turnkeys gaped through the bars that protected them from the rabble. They couldn't believe their eyes. Not a single grimy hand reached out to clutch at her fine, brown woollen gown. No one fought to snatch and claim the gold watch and chain round her neck. They were showing respect for her.

One of the men was so impressed that he brought a chair from the governor's office and opened the gate to pass it through. A prisoner ran forward and he hastily retreated. But she only came to collect the chair and place it behind their visitor for her to sit in.

Elizabeth looked about her and wondered what on earth could be done to help them in such terrible conditions. The only experience she had of the poor people was with their children in her little schools. 'Betsy's Imps', her father called them. She counted the 'Imps' in front of her. There were dozens, because when a mother went into prison she took her children with her. Some were born there. This caused much conflict. Mothers fought for scraps of food for their little ones in order that they would survive. Even worse, some didn't care about their children and would almost steal the food from out of their mouths. In cases like this, the children themselves developed into vicious creatures, as wily as the worst criminals.

All the women stood in silence wondering what she might

say while Elizabeth searched her mind for a solution. Most of all, she wanted to save their souls. If only they would repent of their sins – if they'd committed any in the first place. This would lead them into better lives when they left prison, she thought.

Thinking again of her 'Imps' and remembering William Savery's approach to the Red Indians, she began to ask the young ones some questions.

They knew nothing of reading or writing. Two out of every three grown-ups couldn't read or write. And of those who could, most only knew simple words like dog, cat, mat, sit.

'Would you like me to teach your children to read and write?' she asked.

The women were astounded. Some suspected her intentions. Was she a spy for the authorities? If they said yes, would she report them for making trouble? There had to be an ulterior motive.

She explained that she wanted only to help. If their children were educated, they would stand a better chance in life when they left Newgate. It took a while before they agreed to her suggestion.

That day Elizabeth was only there for a short while. But when she looked back, it seemed like hours. And all because of the awful stench of the filthy room, the unwashed bodies and the rags they wore.

When she was ready to leave, she bade them Goodbye and said she would be back very soon. They didn't believe her, thinking she was only saying that to get away quickly. Forlorn faces pressed up against the metal bars to watch her go and once she was out of their sight they fought like wild she-cats.

The turnkeys were also sure they'd seen the last of Mrs Fry. She'd had her entertainment, watching the miserable creatures in their trap, they thought. True, she had come on a weekday and it was usually Sunday or holidays when the people came to have some fun. And she was different because she'd actually gone into the animals' cage. But that was probably for a dare set by her friends. Now, she'd go and tell everybody how brave she was and how awful they were. Yes, they laughed, she will have a good story to tell when she gets home.

They were right but not in the way they thought.

Elizabeth arrived home feeling very sick. Her clothes, hair and even her skin reeked of the place she'd left. She bathed immediately and put all her clothes in the wash. Although it was January and snowing a servant had to hang the fur-lined cloak and muff out in the garden to sweeten in the fresh air.

'Oh, Joseph, it was far worse than I remembered,' she said, after she'd seen her own little brood warmly tucked in for the night.

She sat in front of a roaring fire, hastily making plans, and Joseph beamed with delight. She was his own Elizabeth again. In that same moment Elizabeth thought so too.

'I've taken the first step along the road to recovery,' she said to herself. Then she gasped as the words repeated themselves in her mind – *a step along the road*. Had the Lord finally made his decision? She was sure he had. Now she was on the right road, after waiting for so long. All her past life had led up to this. It was a form of training: teaching in her own school; ministering in her faith; helping the poor.

'I want thee, Elizabeth Gurney, to be a Light to the Blind; Speech to the Dumb and Feet to the Lame.' She could hear Rebecca young repeating what the Lord had told her.

The blind, the dumb and the lame. This all applied to the miserable people in Newgate. Blind to the written word, dumb with regard to speaking up for themselves and lame when they were unable to walk away from their evil surroundings.

The following day Elizabeth went to see one of her closest friends, Anna Buxton, and told her of Newgate. 'Will you help me, please, Anna?' she asked.

Anna thought for a while. It wasn't the sort of work she felt ladies should do – nor was it the sort of place they should go to. All the same, as a Quaker, it was her duty to serve God and his people.

'I will gladly help thee in any way, Elizabeth,' she answered.

The two women immediately set about collecting, from everyone they knew, cast-off clothing and bedding and especially babies' nappies.

Less than a week later, the two friends were standing outside the prison. Anna shuddered as they approached the high, forbidding walls. But she determined to carry out her promise to help and she said a silent prayer as Elizabeth stepped forward towards the massive oak gates.

This time she brought large containers of hot soup. Her coachman carried them into the prison for her, then hastily ran back to the carriage to wait for her return.

'Oh, no, not you again,' groaned the turnkeys when they saw her walking down the passage from the governor's office. Still, they didn't refuse when she asked them to admit her and to carry the heavy soup containers through the inner gate.

'Pity she's nothing better to idle her time with, silly woman,' one said of the mother of nine children.

'And her husband has no sense, letting her come here,' snarled the other.

Anna was terrified when she saw the dirty, skeletal creatures on the other side of the railings. They looked inhuman. Everything about them was grey – the walls, ceiling and floor; their clothes; even their hair and skin were grey from years of being unwashed. For a few seconds she was unable to move or speak until her friend began to unpack some clean soup bowls she'd brought from home.

Some prisoners sat quietly huddled on piles of dirty straw which served as beds. Refusing to talk to anyone, they stared blankly at the walls or ceiling, trying to shut out of their eyes, ears and minds all the horrors surrounding them. Other prisoners thought they were mad but Anna understood how they felt. She would be like that in a place such as this, she thought.

At the aroma coming from the vegetable soup, the turnkeys were sure there would be a stampede to get at it. Again they were wrong. At Elizabeth's bidding and warm smile, even the quiet, withdrawn ones formed an orderly queue to get their ration. Most of the younger children had never known hot food in their lives.

Prisoners were entitled to a bowl of gruel and a chunk of bread each day, one pound of potatoes each week, and on some days, a small piece of meat. What they actually received were stale crusts that the more wealthy prisoners threw away.

Anyone in prison for an offence other than debt could be a very rich person. Everybody was flung into the same place. But the wealthy ones could get relatives to send good food in to them. They also bribed the turnkeys with ale money to give them the other prisoners' rations. This meant the poorer people were left to starve or fight for any crumbs they could find.

Poor people usually had relatives in prison with them. Because their relations had felt sorry for them being in prison they would steal food and clothes to send to them. In turn, they would be caught and end up there themselves –

often under sentence of death. Stealing could be a hanging offence.

There was no one to keep a check on the turnkeys' behaviour. And any prisoner complaining about ill treatment would only be much worse off afterwards. Prisoners were expected to pay the turnkeys for the very daylight that managed to pierce the tiny, dirty windows.

When their sentence was complete – if they were ever brought to trial in the first place – prisoners had to pay to be released or they would be kept in prison. It was quite common for people found 'not guilty' to stay on in prison until they died if they had no money to pay the turnkeys the release fees they demanded.

In their freedom, many of the Newgate women had worn vivid, fancy clothes and lots of jewellery made from tin or coloured glass. At the sight of the two Plain Quakers, Mrs Fry and her friend, they were overawed. Plain though their dresses were, they could see they were of the finest material and their white caps and neckerchiefs of pure silk. It was clear that they were very wealthy so why should they want to be there? the women wondered. Their gentleness and sincerity and their warm smiles soon chased away the prisoners' suspicions and they ate the soup in silence.

There were three hundred women and children packed into four cells. The entire area was 190 square yards. There were no beds, merely heaps of lice-infested straw which hadn't been changed in years. There were no lavatories, no wash-bowls or water.

Some women had never been brought to trial and couldn't remember when they were arrested. Some didn't know why they had been arrested. Women prisoners were always treated far worse than men. This was because men were expected to have criminal ways. In women it was quite unforgivable.

Elizabeth felt it was very wrong to put two drunken, brutish men in charge of women and children. While the prisoners were eating their soup, she mentioned this to Anna and they had a little discussion. A matron must be brought in to supervise them as soon as possible.

When their meal was over, Elizabeth got all the women to sit or stand round her while she told them of all the ideas in her mind. Her smile and attitude put them at ease. It was as if she were plotting with them against the people who treated them so badly.

First the place must be cleaned up. Buckets, brushes and soap would be provided and everyone would be expected to set to work.

But the prisoners showed no interest in cleanliness. There were many, especially the babies and small children, who had never bathed or even washed in their lives. Elizabeth and Anna convinced them that being clean was a good thing and would make them feel better.

Next she asked if the women could make a little classroom out of one of the four cells for the children.

With three hundred crammed into such a small area they asked how they could afford the space.

They were told that if they could possibly manage it, it wouldn't be for long. Elizabeth was sure that when the authorities saw the prisoners were helping to improve their own conditions, they would be forced into doing something as well. The women agreed. One of the cells would be left empty. It was too little to be missed anyway.

Just as they were leaving, the two Quakers surprised them all when they went on their knees in all the slime and dirt and murmured a prayer for them. To the visitors' surprise, all the women knelt and prayed too.

At the end of that visit, the women of Newgate were confident that Elizabeth would be back. And she'd promised to bring others. She was the one person who gave them any hope, so they needed to put their faith in her.

The governor was extremely shocked at the idea of teaching prisoners' children to read and write. Whenever a letter needed writing, the prisoners paid a few coppers to one who could to write it for them. Even so, hardly any letters were written. 'Who would such people know who could read one?' he asked. No, there was no need to educate the poor. In fact, he believed, it could be dangerous. It encouraged them to think, and thought provoked rebellions.

Elizabeth would hear none of this nonsense. The governor wished she would simply go away and never return. Her ideas were giving him so much trouble.

In the next week, Elizabeth asked several other Quaker friends for help. Among them were the people who first told her of Newgate on the night of the supper party. There was also Samuel Hoare, her younger sister Louisa's husband. He was already very worried about the level of juvenile crime in the country, so he was most eager to assist.

Altogether there were twelve helpers, and they called themselves The Association For The Improvement Of The Female Prisoners In Newgate.

7: The Improvement

Some of Elizabeth's female friends volunteered to accompany her on her visits. Others said nothing could get them near the place, but everyone offered to help in any way they could. They collected all sorts of things, including Bibles. If the children were learning to read, what better book could they have? they asked.

As well as clothing there was a lot of woollen yarn and lengths of material collected. Elizabeth thought that if the women learned to knit and sew, not only would it occupy them, it would provide warm clothing for themselves and their children.

On her next visit to Newgate, she told the women all about the Association formed for their benefit. They began to feel they mattered to the world if others cared about them. Elizabeth was pleased at their attitude. It would help them to change their ways, she was sure, and that was her aim. If they knew total strangers cared for them, wouldn't they soon realise it was the Lord who cared enough to send this help?

Until that time, some of them were so desperate and dejected that with the little money they had, instead of buying food, they bought ale and gin. If they were drunk their troubles were forgotten for a little while. Others gambled for a bit of excitement and the chance to win more money to spend on drink and gambling. Naturally, the Quakers were horrified at both gambling and drunkenness although they approved of alcohol as a medicine.

The first day of change began with a crisp and frosty morning. How eagerly everyone worked. It helped to keep them warm.

Floors were swept before being scrubbed. Some prisoners dragged the damp, foul-smelling straw beds to the gate where Elizabeth instructed the turnkeys to bring pitchforks and remove them from the bulding. Outside in the prison yard was a load of new, yellow straw ready to replace them.

For years, food had been eaten from the tables without so much as a cloth being wiped over them. Green mould and thick grease were ingrained in the wood. No one could believe that, after being thoroughly scrubbed, the wood turned out to be nearly white.

When the cells were clean, they smelled so sweet and looked so bright that they seemed much bigger. Then the women looked at themselves and at their children.

The Quaker helpers said soap and water was coming for them too. After washing they had another surprise: not everyone had grey hair. Some were blonde, others had brown, black and even red hair. A lot of the children didn't know what a comb was. Some had hair so badly infested with lice that it had to be cut off. They were afraid of the scissors too. But once they realised hair-cutting didn't hurt they calmed down. It would soon grow again, they were told, and with all the knots and tangles some would never have got a comb through it anyway. Women offered to have their hair cut off as well to rid them of the lice. Elizabeth promised they would be given little cotton caps similar to her own to cover their heads until it grew again.

All the old rags they'd worn were sent away to be burned and with them the fleas and body lice that bit and itched constantly, causing sores as they were scratched away.

It was strange how the women had stopped swearing, Elizabeth noticed. Not once did she ask them to, although they used the most appalling language. They simply stopped of their own accord as their surroundings improved.

On the first school-day, Elizabeth sat with the children clustered round her in the little classroom that had once been a vile-smelling cell, ankle-deep in filth. How different the place looked in a matter of days. She started by reading a Bible story. When she looked up for a brief pause, she saw that many women were crowded round listening.

When she'd finished, she began a writing lesson on slates with chalk. The women asked if she would teach them too. She hadn't expected that.

That evening she pondered on how to teach three hundred grown-ups and children all at the same time. There was another problem. Elizabeth knew she wasn't the best of teachers. Her own spelling was poor, so was her grammar.

Joseph found the solution. Poor spelling was better than not being able to write at all and she had friends who would help anyway.

'Didn't you say a few of the prison women could read and write? Well, enrol them as teachers too. And another thing, they'll be there in the classroom all the time, even when you're not.'

His wife couldn't wait to get back to Newgate to tell the prisoners what her husband had suggested. There would be classes of twelve people. Each class would have its own teacher who would also be a kind of prefect. It would be her job to hear any complaints or suggestions from the prisoners and then pass them on to Elizabeth on her visits.

Scripture would be read twice each day and while they were listening they could get on with their knitting and sewing. Anyone who didn't know how would be taught by those who could.

What a change the governor saw in Newgate, and it all came about in a matter of a few weeks.

Elizabeth kept reminding him that women prisoners should really be supervised by women. A matron was essential, but he said she was asking too much.

With all the donations of clothing, fabrics and knitting yarn it wasn't long before every prisoner had more clothes than she needed. But as the women enjoyed it, they kept on knitting and sewing until there were many garments left over.

What if they could sell their products to the outside world? Elizabeth thought. That would bring in some money. Then they would really be working for a purpose.

Before long she persuaded some of her Quaker friends with shops to take these garments as part of their stock. Soon the prisoners were delighted to be told they were selling well. Money was beginning to mount up and Elizabeth worried what would happen to it. The turnkeys would soon find ways of taking it from them. So she put forward a proposal that a little shop should be opened in the prison.

Mrs Fry and her work were becoming well known all over the country by this time and the authorities were a little afraid of displeasing her. But with her persuasive voice and her eyes, that were almost hypnotic when she asked a favour of anyone, she usually got her own way. Not only did the prisoners get their shop, they got their matron as well.

Mrs Brown's shop was like Aladdin's Cave to the women in Newgate. She sold coffee, tea, butter, soap, sugar, bread, biscuits and lots of other things, items we take for granted every day. Yet for some of the inmates, they were luxuries many had never seen or tasted in their lives.

It wasn't long before other authorities were asking Mrs Fry's advice on how to improve their own prison conditions for both men and women. Ten months after her first visit to Newgate she was invited to go to the House of Commons to face a committee which wished to question her about her work and its value.

She was asked if she found the women clean and industrious. Of course they were, she replied. It was thanks to her and not the law of the land, nor the rules of Newgate. But she didn't say that.

She told them of how the women were making and selling thousands of garments and knitting thousands of pairs of socks which were sold in shops for two shillings a pair (10p).

The committee said this was taking work away from respectable people who weren't in prison.

She answered that prisoners had as much right as anyone else to work and earn a bit of money. It gave them a feeling of dignity and urged them to be better people.

Didn't they spend it on drink and gambling? they asked.

Elizabeth told them about Mrs Brown's shop. They already knew about it and had led her into a trap.

Weren't coffee, tea, butter and other such things too good for such awful creatures? they asked.

Elizabeth controlled her anger and gently explained that she didn't believe prison should be a place solely for punishment. It should be a place where they would be reformed.

At the end of the meeting she left for home knowing she had stated her case and they had agreed with everything she said.

Although she was a very kindhearted person, Elizabeth was never opposed to punishment for wrongdoers. She was opposed, though, to the sort of punishment they often received.

People could be hanged for smuggling, forgery, stealing

cattle, chopping down trees, poaching, shoplifting or stealing anything at all that was worth more than a shilling (5p). Very young children could be condemned to death – and it was usually for stealing food because they were starving. They were nearly always reprieved. Still, they had to suffer the terror of being condemned, not knowing if they would hang or not.

For offences committed in prison, such as complaining of bad treatment or hunger or for fighting with other prisoners for the food and clothes they'd had stolen from them, it could mean solitary confinement. This was in rat-infested, windowless dungeons, down in the dank earth way below the prison itself. The offenders were often shackled in irons to the dungeon walls and left there for very long periods. Some went mad, others died from cold, fear or both.

Elizabeth appealed to the Home Secretary to have this stopped. Solitary confinement could still be used for very serious offences but only for a few days and in an ordinary cell.

She made her own rules for punishing prisoners' children who misbehaved. They were to clean and sew from morning till night until they were sorry. To us this seems harsh but remember, children worked from dawn till dusk in mills and mines.

Around that time, an eleven-year-old girl in Scotland was asked about her work. She said that she worked all day, bent double carrying trays of coal to the bottom of the pit shaft. The tray was strapped to her back and held one hundred-weight of coal.

One newspaper of the day was publishing readers' letters advising on how best to beat young daughters. Some parents thought it better to use birch twigs. Others thought it better to strip them and beat them with a leather belt. By comparison, Elizabeth's chastisement seems quite lenient.

After her visit to the House of Commons—which the whole country heard about—more and more people approached her who were eager to help improve the prisons.

Within a year those who used to go there for amusement had lost all interest. With no filth, fighting, starvation, swearing, screaming or brutality from the drunken turnkeys, it wasn't fun any more.

Instead they saw the women, all clean and tidy, sitting sewing or knitting while Mrs Fry and her ladies from The Association For The Improvement Of The Female Prisoners In Newgate read them stories from the Bible.

But there was a sad side to all Elizabeth's good work—transportation.

As long as the women were in prison, she could help them. As soon as they sailed on board a convict ship there was nothing she could do.

The journey to Botany Bay was so long and so terrible that some didn't survive. Those who did soon forgot all they'd learned and ended up as bad as, if not worse than before they ever went to Newgate.

8: Convict Ships and Workhouses

As far back as medieval times, European countries were shipping their criminals out to populate new lands they had conquered. Prisoners sentenced to hang could sometimes choose transportation rather than be put to death.

Some of the crimes which led to their having to make this choice have already been mentioned. But there were so many, including receiving stolen goods (fencing); stealing metal or timber; stealing people's letters; stealing from lodgings; poaching fish from rivers or ponds, or poaching game from fields and woods; assault with intent to rob; bigamy; forgery and many, many others.

Murder and manslaughter were the most serious of all crimes. They were probably the only ones deserving of such harsh punishment; even so, hanging was a great improvement on earlier times when murderers were boiled alive. Political and religious offenders were sent on the convict ships. So were felons guilty of the most petty crimes, even by the rigid standards of those times.

By Elizabeth Fry's day it was usually only second offenders who were subjected to this punishment, but not always. Giving false information on birth, marriage or death certificates carried a sentence of seven years' transportation. And today, in parts of England, there are ancient bridges still displaying old warning notices that anyone damaging the bridge will be transported for life.

In the years just before Elizabeth was born it was mostly to America that England sent her convicts to work on the plantations. But after 1782 and the War of Independence, America refused to have them.

As there was nowhere else suitable for them to go, the prisons gradually became overcrowded. To make room in them, the government decided to use the convict ships as extra prisons. They were old and their timbers rotting. All the same, they were moored in the River Thames and filled with the prisoners who would have been transported, had there been a place to send them. Naturally, it wasn't long before they were overcrowded too.

For a long time, the government had been thinking of using Botany Bay as a convict settlement. When Captain Cook explored Australia in 1770, he claimed the east coast for Britain. The native Aborigines, who were much friendlier than the American Red Indians, were few in number, and so it was a vast, underpopulated land. Australia was also on the far side of the world, which was where the authorities wanted their criminals to be – as far away as possible.

Only one thing was stopping them. At £28 each, the cost to Botany Bay – now called Sydney – was far more than it had been to America. Keeping prisoners on the old vessels in the Thames for a whole year cost only £10 per person for food and clothing, which they hardly ever saw anyway.

Still, with the ships becoming overcrowded, something needed to be done. To build more prisons would be even more expensive than the £28 to Botany Bay. And so it was settled that they must be sent to Australia. The first 800 to go set sail in 1785, just about the time the Gurneys were moving into Earlham Hall.

Unseaworthy though the old transporters were, it was these rotting hulks which were put under sail for the long voyage. Many prisoners failed to arrive there because of the conditions on board. Seasickness was the least of their troubles. Heartless ship's captains and sadistic turnkeys could treat them in any way they liked. No one cared about the prisoners' welfare.

For the slightest misdemeanour, a convict could be severely flogged, put into chains and thrown into a cell. These were often below the ship's waterline and in rough seas it wasn't unknown for the poor wretches to drown in their cells.

Keel-hauling was a terrible punishment, when a prisoner was tied to a rope, thrown overboard and drawn under the ship to be hauled up on the other side. If he didn't drown he usually died from injuries received when smashing against the ship's side or the keel. Hanging from the yard-arm wasn't always reserved for mutineers or pirates either.

When they arrived at Botany Bay, any who did survive the tortuous voyage were sent to work for the farmers or other settlers until their sentence was done. The usual time was seven years, although it could be for life. While serving their sentences they were in 'bondage' to their employers. This was a sort of slavery with pay. But when their sentence was over they were released from bondage to become free men.

I say men because people rarely employed women. They wanted nothing to do with a woman criminal.

When women arrived in Australia they were given no shelter, merely a small sum of money to buy food. This would be spent on some form of shelter, particularly by the mothers with small children and babies. Then they were left either to starve or steal again for food. This resulted in further punishment. And remember, these women had probably never stolen or committed any crime in their lives.

Many of the men pitied them, especially those who had left penniless wives and children at home in England. As they were stronger, sometimes they would built a bit of shelter for them. Others worked longer hours to make extra money to give to them, while others simply stole food or money from their employers to give to the starving women. Then they were in more trouble when they were discovered.

As time went on, Australia became more and more populated with sheep-farmers providing meat and arable farmers growing food. Then the British government found it cheaper to sent criminals to Botany Bay because it didn't need to ship food out to them.

Once a convict was released from his bondage he was free to return to England. This meant finding a ship's captain who was looking for an extra crew member for the journey home. The former prisoner would have no money to pay for his fare, which was beyond the means of most people.

Knowing this, the British government offered small areas of land to those who couldn't get back to England. And, after many years in Australia, some of them didn't want to come back as they'd made new lives for themselves in a new land.

How the sight of women prisoners sentenced to, or choosing, transportation distressed Elizabeth Fry. Chained together, they were driven to the docks through the streets in open wagons, their weeping, terrified children beside them. That was bad enough without having to face the jeering crowds who threw rotten eggs, fruit and vegetables at them as they passed by. Once on board ship, they were roughly pushed below decks. Sometimes they were on board for weeks until the ship was fully loaded and ready to sail.

On one occasion, when Elizabeth went to say farewell to some of the Newgate women, another group of women from a different prison arrived at the dockside. One woman was shuffling along to the accompaniment of harsh words and prods from a brutish-looking turnkey. The woman was crying out and obviously was in great pain. When Elizabeth stepped forward to see what was the cause, she was sickened.

Iron fetters round the woman's ankles had cut deep into the flesh. Her feet and legs were so badly swollen that the irons were barely visible. Elizabeth was so enraged that she gripped the turnkey's arm and demanded that the irons be removed immediately. The other officials present were so afraid of her anger and in awe of her reputation that they obeyed her order. As the cruel irons were cut away, the woman fainted and had to be carried aboard.

Mrs Fry wasted no time in contacting the authorities. She insisted that in future no women would be shackled, nor would they be taken to the docks in open wagons. Only closed carriages must be used. Furthermore, she intended to go with them, not just to the dockside but on to the vessels to check the conditions on board. She would also pay them frequent visits while they were waiting to sail.

With her growing fame, no one dared to defy her and from then until shortly before she died, Elizabeth regularly visited every single convict ship until it sailed.

The members of the Association For The Improvement Of The Female Prisoners In Newgate were her greatest allies in this. In the long weeks on board while waiting for the ships to sail, the prisoners were given work to do and the lessons went on as usual. When they were ready to leave Newgate for the docks, the Association presented each woman with a little gift parcel. In each was an apron and cap, sewing and knitting equipment, a bundle of fabrics to make patchwork with, a pair of scissors, a comb, knife, fork and spoon and above all, a Bible. Some had never owned so much in their lives and most had never owned a book of any kind, let alone a Bible, which they were now able to read themselves.

The saddest part of all was knowing that, once they were at sea, there was no one to care for them. The real criminals, who were beginning to reform before they left, usually ended up as bad as or worse than they were in the first place. Any who were just beginning to put their faith in mankind and, above all, in God, felt abandoned and their faith soon died.

By this time everyone in the land – and in Europe – had heard about Mrs Fry and her good work. Other prison governors and committees were inviting her to their prisons and sometimes their lunatic asylums to advise them on how to improve their conditions. This made her very happy but at the same time she was getting those guilty feelings again.

The strictest of the Quaker elders were in no doubt that she was neglecting her husband and children. Her place was in the home, like all wives and mothers. But Elizabeth wasn't away from home every day, and certainly never in the evening. There were servants and nannies in the house all the time. Still, she worried so much over the criticism that her nerves started to trouble her. She tried reassuring herself that God would never have led her to Newgate if she were doing wrong. And it was God who led her into her marriage with Joseph, something which had made them both extremely happy.

Joseph told her that if he approved of what she was doing, she shouldn't concern herself with what others thought. It didn't stop her from lying awake worrying most nights, and especially after a hard day's work.

There was so much reform to do all over the world, and

Elizabeth felt she should do her share of it in London. Plashet House in Essex was within reasonable travelling distance from the city and, of course, when they were staying at Mildreds Court, either for the Quarterly Meeting or in the wintertime, that was even closer to Newgate and her work.

But what am I going to do about all these invitations? she wondered. Eventually, she decided to visit the places close to home and in other parts of London.

The conditions in most of these other prisons were as bad as, sometimes worse than Newgate had been such a short time before. And once again, the criminals weren't really criminals at all in the majority of cases.

In one prison she met a seventeen-year-old boy. He was well-spoken and well-mannered. His few remnants of clothing were of good quality. When Elizabeth asked why he was there he told her of his terrible crime. His employer had taken him before a Court of Justice and accused him of being 'an idler and a daydreamer'. For this he was sent to prison.

Elizabeth thought back to her youth, when she could have been accused of the same crime. There were even a couple of daydreamers among her own children.

In the century before Elizabeth was born it was enough to accuse someone of witchcraft to have them arrested, tortured and executed. In the eighteenth and nineteenth centuries, when the world was becoming more 'civilised', it was sufficient to accuse someone of theft for them to be carried off to prison, often in chains. If anyone bothered to bring them to trial it wasn't always a good thing. They could face a bench of drunken magistrates whose only qualification to judge others was that they were wealthy landowners. The prisoner could easily be sentenced to death or transportation and have no appeal.

Female domestic servants and shop assistants were at most risk. An employer only needed to misplace something to accuse the girl of stealing it. The object could be found later but nothing would be done to help the girl who was languishing in gaol. It would never occur to her accuser to apologise and admit there had been a mistake. In fact, these heartless people seriously believed a long spell in prison or a convict settlement was good for the poor. It would teach them a lesson – just in case they were ever tempted to steal.

Of course, there were very few employers like that. The majority were very kind and cared for their workers but those with villainous natures knew they had the wealth and power to do as they liked.

One of Elizabeth's worst experiences was meeting a young mother who had stolen a piece of cloth worth five shillings (25p) and sold it to buy food for her children. She was sentenced to hang and was heartbroken at leaving her little ones to the mercy of the world.

Her husband wasn't dead, nor had he deserted them. He'd been press-ganged into the navy. Young men living in dockside areas went about in fear of this fate. They could leave their homes to go on an errand or to their work and never be seen again. Whenever a ship was short of crewmen, the captain could legally pay gangs of men to get the necessary manpower by press-ganging. Armed and carrying warrants, they could waylay and seize any able-bodied man on the street and take him aboard the ship which would be ready to sail on the tide.

The man could be carried off to foreign lands and his family would never know what had happened to him, unless someone more fortunate had witnessed the press-ganging. His wife and children were simply left to fend for themselves or starve. As fending for themselves meant stealing or begging for food they would end up in prison, because begging was just as serious a crime as stealing.

There were always the workhouses where poor people could go to live. But these were terrible places. No matter how awful a person's home was – a hovel with bare walls and earth floor, no furniture, and straw for beds – they would struggle to survive and stay there rather than go into the workhouse. With luck, a man could always poach fish or game to feed his family and collect firewood for heat without being caught, and live in freedom. There was no freedom in the workhouse. Families were split up as men, women and children were all separated and housed in different wings of the great, bleak buildings. They were given very little food and clothing and there was practically no heating.

The people in charge of these places could be every bit as cruel as prison turnkeys. The one difference was that the buildings were spotlessly clean and so were the people who lived there. This was because everyone, even the sick and elderly, was forced to scrub the floors, walls and furniture and wash clothes every day until their hands were raw and bleeding and their strength gave out. All this harsh treatment was to stop people from wanting to go into the workhouse, and it was successful.

As in prison, inmates were punished for the most trifling things. The most usual form of punishment was to miss their meals, but some places had dungeons where offenders would be shut up for hours or days.

Children rarely survived long. Any baby born there wasn't expected to live more than a few weeks. They were taken from their mothers soon after birth and put into the children's wing. There 'nurses', as they called themselves, often simply neglected them and left them to die because babies were a lot of work.

Perhaps they were fortunate. The children, especially little boys, who did survive the horrors of the workhouse were the unlucky ones. At four years of age, orphan boys could be sold to work in mines or mills where they often got tangled up in the heavy machinery to be maimed or killed.

The worst fate of all was to be bought by a chimney-sweep. He needed very small boys to climb up the inside of, quite often, still hot chimneys in mansion houses, halls and manors. It was his task to sweep down the choking, black soot and it was very common for a child to get stuck up there. The cure was to light the fire under him. This was supposed to make him quickly find a way of getting unstuck. It usually resulted in his being severely burned, sometimes to death.

It was easy to pick out a sweep's boy. He would be covered in cuts and bruises and sores from always rubbing against the rough brickwork inside the chimneys. Soot would get into the open wounds and they would heal, leaving a coal-black scar.

A sweep could get nearly a year's work out of a small boy before he died. Then he would return to the workhouse to buy another.

9: Travels and Tears

1818 saw Elizabeth in her thirty-eighth year and with family worries. Not only did her children bear the same names as their Gurney aunts and uncles, they were displaying all the same signs of bad behaviour.

Throughout the week their father was working at his bank while their mother was either teaching in her school in the grounds behind Plashet House, doing some sort of charity work for the poor or visiting Newgate and the convict ships in London.

Elizabeth remembered how rebellious the Gurney children became after their mother, Catherine, died and she couldn't help comparing the circumstances. Was she neglecting her family duties as some suggested she was? she wondered. This would put her children into a similar situation as when she, her brothers and her sisters lost their mother.

She made herself quite ill with worry and prayed late into the night when everyone was asleep. She asked the Lord if it was his wish that she give up her work. But then, she argued with herself, wouldn't I be neglecting my duty to him?

Despite the Society of Friends' criticism of her, it was through them that the Lord gave his answer. Until then, even though she was a respected Quaker minister, because of her domestic ties, the Friends had never asked her to travel to Meeting Houses away from home. But as she could find time for interests they didn't approve of, was it unreasonable for them to expect her to do what they would approve of? they wondered.

The Society's General Meeting was to take place in August. Elizabeth's younger brother, Joseph Gurney, was invited to go and the Society thought it time Elizabeth should do her duty and attend with him.

She didn't mind going to the General Meeting but she was faced with one very important problem. It was to be held in Aberdeen, Scotland – 600 miles from her home, her family and her work.

At that time her own little school would be closed for the summer break. The prison visits near home could be taken care of by all the helpers she'd recruited over the years. Her greatest worry was over leaving Joseph and the children.

The two older boys, John and William, were at boarding-school. But in early July, just when she would be starting her long journey to Scotland, they would be home for the holidays. The younger children's school lessons at home would be finishing too.

Again it was Joseph who found the solution. All the children could be sent on holiday to various relatives, some to their Uncle Joe's home, Earlham, where Aunt Janet and their cousins would gladly welcome them, some to the Fry relations, and others to Elizabeth's sisters and brothers who lived about the area between Norwich and London. It would be a nice change for them and would leave their mother free from worry.

Elizabeth agreed with her husband and yet she felt so wretched at leaving them. She didn't complain, though. She would be carrying out her duty to God and to the Society of Friends.

She adored her handsome younger brother. Like her he had become a Plain Quaker some years earlier and wouldn't have been recognised as the unruly, mischievous little boy of the past.

During their planning for the journey, Elizabeth decided it would be a good opportunity to accept some of the many invitations sent to her by prison governors and others from all over the country. Her brother suggested they should visit several Meeting Houses while they were travelling too. As the name of Elizabeth Fry was so well known, everyone would want to meet her, he thought.

His sister felt he might be right, but as pride was never supposed to enter a Quaker mind she kept her thoughts to herself.

From London to Aberdeen was a long and tedious journey in the days of coach and horses. Elizabeth, never knowing good health, was sometimes travel-sick, and during that hot summer she often felt faint too.

There must have been times on that gruelling journey when she looked back with longing to the cool, leafy gardens of Earlham Park. To the days when she wandered there, carefree and bonnet-free with the little brother who was now taking care of her so well.

Joseph Gurney was very concerned for his sister and wondered if the Friends had been wise. Perhaps someone more robust should have been chosen.

They were both grateful for the lengthy stops made on the way, although each stop involved strenuous prison visits and long Meetings in gloomy, airless Meeting Houses. Some towns gave them civic receptions at Town Halls and they were often invited to the homes of local dignitaries.

Going north they stayed at Lincoln, Sheffield, Doncaster, Wakefield, Leeds, York, Darlington, Durham, Newcastle, Berwick, Dunbar and finally arrived at Aberdeen. By now, Elizabeth was so famous that everywhere they went, people, not only Quaker Friends, were eager to accompany her to the various prisons she visited. And it was an easy task to persuade them to keep up with the visits after Elizabeth had gone on her way.

Some of the prisons were well run, with their inmates well cared for, clean and actually receiving all the food and clothing they were entitled to. Others were even worse than Newgate had been. This was because each local authority was responsible for its own prisons, and sense of responsibility varied from town to town.

Although they had invited her, some prison governors were displeased when, on arrival, she explained that she didn't want to question them about the prison. It was the prisoners themselves she wanted to talk to.

The prisoners were always amazed when Elizabeth walked in amongst them. There she stood, calm and smiling. In her plain gown and shawl with her linen cap only partly covering her lustrous golden hair, she shone like an angel in their miserable surroundings. Many had never heard of Mrs Fry and were suspicious of her. But like the Newgate women, when they heard the musical tones of her voice and saw how gentle her manner was, it was as if a spell was cast and they were eager to listen to her. When she knelt on the cold stone floor, clasped her hands and closed her eyes in prayer to pray 'for us', they were in tears.

Never did she speak of their crimes. Only of 'our sins' and of how the Lord wants to 'help us' to lead better lives. It was always as though she were one of them and not someone better.

Before leaving, Elizabeth always asked if they would like visits from ladies of their own town to read to them, or maybe teach some to read and write, especially their children.

In every town committees and organisations in all faiths were set up. There were Quakers, Roman Catholics,

Presbyterians and some of no religious belief. All showed willing to help others, through either their wealth or influence. Some would merely collect food, clothing or soap and others would provide them with some form of occupation. Most of all, in place of drunken, cruel louts, there would be good, decent people found to supervise the prisoners.

Joseph Gurney became involved in his sister's work too and together they visited men's and women's prisons and lunatic asylums. Whenever they attended Friends' Meeting Houses both brother and sister would speak during the silence.

It was two months after setting off from London and after attending the Friends' General Meeting in Aberdeen that they began their journey home. This took a whole month. Again they stayed at different places on the way south, Edinburgh, Glasgow, Manchester. The bumpy roads rocked the carriage and there were times when they were forced to halt by the wayside to rest because Elizabeth felt ill.

A year earlier, she had received an invitation from the Earl of Derby to visit his home in the north of England, Knowsley Hall near Liverpool in Lancashire.

Despite Elizabeth's Plain Quaker simplicity, she could never resist high-ranking people, statesmen or anyone famous. Most of all she was drawn to royalty and the nobility. She tried hard to keep this weakness hidden but it often crept up to show itself on the surface. Just before setting out for Scotland, she'd written to the Earl accepting his invitation, and on the way home from Aberdeen she and her brother went to Knowsley.

What a grand reception awaited them. It was such a welcome relief from the squalor and misery they'd seen over the past weeks in prisons and asylums.

The Earl was entertaining many guests at the Hall that week. It was so long since Elizabeth had seen such a display that she was quite bedazzled by all the jewels and finery. The company treated Elizabeth and her brother as though they themselves were royalty. Joseph humbly accepted it out of courtesy, but it was strongly against his Quaker ideals.

In contrast to him, Elizabeth's heart danced and her eyes sparkled with delight, especially when everyone marched in grand procession to the magnificent dining-hall, she leading the way, arm-in-arm with Lady Derby.

At thirty-eight, Elizabeth was still very beautiful if a little rounder than the slim girl she'd once been. In her demure green velvet gown with her white silk neck shawl and ruched bonnet with its green velvet band, she somehow stood out amidst all the grandeur of the old Hall and the Earl's guests.

Later that evening she asked her brother, 'Joseph, did I behave in an unbecoming manner today?'

He thought she hadn't but she was unconvinced. She was aware that, after supper, when she led them all in prayer, against everything she believed in she relished being the object of everyone's attention.

Pride and vanity had overwhelmed her, and Elizabeth was filled with remorse. Disregarding all the hard work and the discomfort she'd endured on their tour from one end of the island to the other, she felt she'd now sinned. Kneeling beside her bed, she prayed for forgiveness from the Lord for yielding to her 'poor womanly weakness'.

Without realising it, Joseph had felt pride in his heart for his sister on that day. Later, when he remarked on how her simple sincerity influenced and outshone everyone they met, Elizabeth squirmed inside. She tried to feel meek, but deep inside there was still the excitement of being fêted at all the Town Halls and private homes they'd been to, particularly the most recent grand reception at Knowsley.

Elizabeth was deeply distressed on arriving home to find her husband lying ill and to hear he had forbidden anyone to write and let her know. Seventeen-year-old Kate, left as mistress of the house in her mother's absence, was ill and so too was four-year-old Louisa.

How their mother blamed herself for leaving them and fussed around her invalids. When the other children began to arrive home from their stays with other relatives, Elizabeth realised how much she'd missed them. And they'd missed her too. There were many tears and hugs. But their coming home was going to give them just time to prepare for the new school term and the family would only have a few days together.

Elizabeth's three months away from home gave her critics in the Society of Friends something substantial to complain about. They had asked her to go to Aberdeen but it was her own idea to stay away so long.

The Frys had stayed at Mildreds Court in Elizabeth's absence. Now she was determined to make up for all the summer months they'd been apart. She ordered the entire household to be packed up and everyone returned to Plashet House in the tranquil Essex countryside. There they could all be together in peace for what was left of the school holidays, and she could devote her time to nursing her sick husband and the two girls.

She put so much into this that she soon fell ill herself. Three months of constant travelling with lengthy spells of work in between had taken their toll of her health. It took the whole of the winter and the following spring for her to recover, and Elizabeth really believed it was God's way of punishing her for that splendid day at Knowsley Hall.

When summer returned, Elizabeth was determined it

would be different from the previous year. They all went to stay at Broadstairs in Kent, where they spent a lovely holiday with perfect weather.

Every day was spent idly wandering along the beach collecting colourful, rounded pebbles or sea-shells – the collection she'd wanted so much as a child and always been afraid to make. Sometimes they all sat listening to and watching the changing tides as the sea alternately lapped and spumed against the shore.

Towards the end of autumn the family moved up to Mildreds Court again for the harsh winter lying ahead. The serenity of the summer was soon forgotten when Elizabeth's hectic life began again.

First came a letter from a Reverend Samuel Marsden who lived in Australia. He was concerned for the female convicts there. Elizabeth was always thinking about them and their children who were transported with them. Once the ships sailed they were out of her reach. Whatever influence she had with the British authorities, she had none at all with those in far-off Australia.

Mr Marsden knew of her good work in Britain and said it was heartbreaking to see it all go to waste. When the prisoners arrived in Botany Bay most of them fell into crime through starvation and neglect.

Years before, he'd sailed on a convict ship when he was going to settle in Australia. He'd seen what happened to the women on their arrival and ever since he'd been trying to get a hostel for them to live in. In desperation, he wrote to Mrs Fry to see if she could help. He told of how some women were bought as wives for soldiers or other convicts. At least this provided them with food and shelter. But it was a situation no one should be forced into, he said. If only there were a hostel for them to live in when they arrived, with a team of supervisors to watch over them and perhaps find them work.

Elizabeth was overjoyed at this suggestion and sent letters of support for Samuel Marsden to the authorities in Australia. She also wrote to the good man himself advising him on what a hostel should provide and how it would best be run. By that time Mrs Fry's name was becoming well known in Australia, and within a short time the hostel was built.

Next came letters from Russia. Their prisons and lunatic asylums were far worse than anything in Britain. In disbelief of what she heard, the Russian Empress herself went to visit them. As a result, plans for new prison buildings were made and sent to England for Elizabeth's approval. She immediately set about altering them as they had asked her to do if she thought they were wrong. Elizabeth added wings to too small buildings and drew windows in where none were planned.

She told them that lunatics should not be treated like criminals. They were sick and needed care, not punishment. On hearing this, the Russian Empress insisted they be taken care of just like hospital patients. They were given proper clothes, sat at table for meals and were allowed to use knives, forks and spoons.

Within the space of a few years, Russia's mentally ill were receiving the best treatment in the world. No longer were they thought of as wicked or as a source of entertainment for the sane. Yet here in Britain they were still being treated that way in many places.

While Elizabeth was helping and advising other countries with similar requests she was very busy on another project here at home.

The year before had seen a cold and blustery autumn, resulting in many lost harvests. The winter that followed was so cold that in the mornings, after terribly severe frosty nights, poor, homeless people were found frozen to death in the streets.

Two of Elizabeth's brothers-in-law, Fowell Buxton and Samuel Hoare, Hannah's and Louisa's husbands, already served on the committee of the Association For The Improvement Of The Female Prisoners In Newgate. Elizabeth asked if they would help form another committee to collect a sum of money in aid of London's homeless. They did, and with it they bought an old disused mill. This gave shelter to many who would no doubt have lost their lives in the freezing night temperatures.

Shortly afterwards, Fowell's little boy fell ill. Within three days three more of his children took to their beds. As their father was busily involved with the shelter for the homeless, trying to get fuel and food for it, Elizabeth packed a few bags and moved into his home. Her sister Hannah was thankful for her help in nursing her little ones. No one thought the children were seriously ill at first. But six days later all four were dead and their parents were so distraught that they too fell ill.

Fowell was completely bewildered. Why had the Lord done this to him? he asked again and again. Hadn't he spent all the winter helping to save the lives of others?

Very gently, his sister-in-law told him it wasn't for him to question the ways of the Lord. His little ones had died from an illness man had no cure for. But hadn't they lived and died in a home full of love, warmth and comfort? So unlike the little ones who would have died in the London streets without his help.

Before the winter was over, Elizabeth was called to Norwich where her young sister, Priscilla, lay ill. She too died and Elizabeth became deeply depressed at all the tragedy around her. It seemed as if the family would never know happiness again.

As the winter eased into spring, Joseph could see that she was pining just as when their own little girl had died three years before. Newgate was the cure then. What is the answer this time, Lord? he asked.

The Lord answered him when he sent her brother, Joseph, to see her. He asked if she would help him to write a book telling of their experiences on their tour of England and Scotland. All who read it would be shocked into knowing what was happening in their own country. Powerful and rich people would read it and be moved to offer their assistance.

Elizabeth was full of enthusiasm. Without such a book how could those who didn't visit prisons discover the truth and the horrors of such places?

There was so much the world should know: of men in chains spending months in cold, dark, dirty dungeons. There was an Aberdeen prison where a whole family of five lived in one room with only two heaps of verminous straw for beds. A very sick man and a tiny child lay in one bed while an old bedridden woman lay coughing her life away in the other.

At one prison in Scotland there was a young man who was clearly mentally retarded. At the time of her visit he had been kept in a dungeon in solitary confinement for eighteen months. And his dreadful crime? He had damaged a park bench.

Often, where prisoners were kept in irons, the chain was looped through a ring set in the wall. To release them a blacksmith had to be employed, and it was usually because the victim had died.

Did the public know what sort of people were put in charge of prisons? They were not intelligent, well-trained supervisors with the prisoners' welfare at heart. Brutal, ignorant drunks were chosen for their hardness and lack of feeling.

In one prison Elizabeth and Joseph saw a notice pinned to a wall which read:

The Rules of this Room for everyman that come
in this to pay 3d for Cols Sticks and Candels
When you fust com in Tow Men to Clenthis Room
and the youngest Prisoner to do anything that is arsk
Any one
that is cort polan this down will
have three donson

The notice is difficult though not impossible to read. 'Cols Sticks and Candels' of course meant coal, firewood and candles. 3d (1½p) was a lot of money then – if the prisoners had any money at all. 'Three donson' – or dozen, as it should read – would mean lashes.

A Yorkshire prison that was built to hold 100 people was actually housing 1,600 men and 300 women.

There was the prison where fifteen men lived in one cell. They were given firewood and 8d (3½p) a day between them. But there was no soap, no clothes for them and nothing for them to do. Another prison had women living and sleeping in one small cell and never going outside for exercise throughout their sentences.

Compiling the book helped Elizabeth to overcome the great sadness her Gurney relatives had just endured. The book was a great success. On publication, the British government was full of praise and so were all the European governments. Invitations were sent for her to go and inspect the prisons of Italy, France, Denmark, Holland, Belgium, Switzerland and Russia.

This made Elizabeth feel quite satisfied with the task, but there was another sadness about to face her. At eighteen, her daughter Rachel had fallen in love with Francis Creswell, a non-Quaker, and they wanted to marry.

To marry a non-Quaker was quite unforgivable in the eyes of the Society of Friends. Not only would Rachel be expelled from the Society, but they would elder her parents – and her mother was an elder herself. As a Quaker minister, Elizabeth wouldn't be allowed to attend her own daughter's wedding.

Rachel argued that her aunts Richenda, Hannah and Louisa had all married 'out', as the Friends called it. They were all good Christians and their marriages were perfectly happy. Elizabeth could only agree with her.

Richenda's husband, Francis Cunningham, was an Anglican clergyman. Fowell Buxton and Samuel Hoare, Hannah's and Louisa's husbands, were non-Quakers, and they were Elizabeth's and Joseph's closest friends. Indeed it was these three men who had done more than anyone to provide the London shelter for the homeless.

Elizabeth remembered the sadness when her favourite sister, Rachel, had fallen in love with Henry Enfield all those years ago. Rachel never did marry. In her heart, Elizabeth didn't understand why people should make so much fuss over anyone marrying 'out'. She certainly couldn't see why the Quaker partner in such a marriage should be expelled from the Society. Still, that was the rule, and, as a minister, she above all must respect it, she decided.

When he heard of it, young Rachel's uncle, Francis Cunningham, offered to marry her and Francis Creswell in his own church in Norwich. There was nothing else her parents could do but accept the situation, and Elizabeth offered to help Rachel select her trousseau.

Unlike her mother, Rachel was to have a grand Church of England ceremony. Most of her Gurney aunts and uncles and cousins would be there. Her wedding gown was to be highly ornamented with lace and frills. Her trousseau consisted of jewels and furs, silks, satins, velvets and laces of every rainbow hue. How Elizabeth secretly enjoyed doing this motherly 'duty'. She loved to handle the beautiful clothes as they arrived and were put into Rachel's bedroom.

But there was sorrow mingled with the joy. Her first child to be married, and she couldn't be present at the wedding.

At last, when the time came for the family to leave for Norwich, her mother declined to go. She wasn't sure she could trust herself to stay at Earlham on the wedding day instead of going along to the church. She chose to stay at Plashet House, and on the wedding day, August 23rd, a day which should have been one of her happiest, she spent her time in her normal work.

When Joseph Gurney heard that his dear sister Betsy was expecting another baby he was very concerned for her health and indeed her life. She was forty-two years of age and in delicate health. He begged the Lord to spare her and wrote frequently asking her to give up her Newgate visits until after the baby was born.

Sadly, it was Jane, his own wife, who died suddenly that June. Elizabeth had always felt more of a mother to Joseph than a sister, and when she heard the sad news her heart ached for him and his children. She set off for Earlham at once to offer him as much comfort and help as she could.

She gave birth to her eleventh child, Daniel, on the same day that young Rachel's first baby was born. The family found it amusing that Rachel's baby would have an uncle of the same age.

Only eight weeks after that November day, although the January snow lay on the ground, Elizabeth had a yearning to go to Newgate. It seemed so long since her last visit in the autumn. How surprised the matron and the prisoners were when she arrived with her tiny new baby in her arms.

Daniel was so snugly wrapped against the cold that his little face could barely be seen. Still, taking a baby in there was something she would never have dreamed of doing when she first set foot in Newgate.

Now the prison was a different world. Its inmates were so clean and well-behaved that it was hard to remember it as it was. Together they all knelt and prayed for the souls of babies everywhere, and then proud mothers came forward with their own children to peer at little Daniel Fry.

As soon as he was weaned from his mother she was back in the midst of all her work again, sitting on committees, organising Sales of Work for the poor, attending meetings with all sorts of officials who were involved in social reform. She was also travelling more now to attend Friends' Meeting Houses and visit prisons further away from home.

All this was in addition to seeing to her husband, her young children and her home. But now she had Catherine. Not only was Catherine like her aunt in being known as Kate. Just as Kate Gurney had taken over the running of Earlham Hall when her mother died, Kate Fry was housekeeper at Plashet House. This helped her mother enormously, and none of the family resented her leaving them for a short while when they had their big sister to take care of them.

10: Elizabeth in Disgrace

Everyone sought Elizabeth's advice and help, even following her to her home in Essex or when she was staying at Mildreds Court during the winter months.

There were ex-prisoners, poor people, church representatives from all faiths, even clients from her husband's bank when they had personal problems they thought she could solve.

Regarding her husband and his bank, Elizabeth had her own personal problems. Unfortunately, Joseph Fry was a much better husband and father than he was a businessman. He loved to spend money and his wife was always worrying over his extravagances. Apart from the amount of money he readily parted with, she felt he didn't show the restraint a Plain Quaker should towards splendour and costly possessions.

She often hinted that he spent too much money. And yet, loving him as she did, she refrained from criticising him too much because of her own guilt. Believing she was a neglectful wife and mother, Elizabeth didn't think she was in any position to find fault with him.

No matter what she did she felt unworthy as a person and was always asking God to forgive her for not doing enough for him. Not content with being a wife and a mother to ten children, Elizabeth seemed to want to mother the whole world. This wasn't humanly possible but Elizabeth despised herself for not having the ability and felt she'd failed in her duty to God.

In the years following Daniel's birth, Elizabeth Fry established so many different charities and organisations that it would take a separate book to list and describe them all.

One was a 'savings society' which encouraged people to set aside a few coppers each week. One of her helpers would call round to collect them and keep them safe until they mounted up to a considerable sum. Until then, the poor had always believed savings were something reserved for the rich. How their attitude to life changed when they saw two farthings grow to a halfpenny and then to pennies and shillings. To have £1 in savings gave them dignity and an independence they'd never imagined.

There was another excellent organisation to improve the working and living conditions of domestic servants, and another to provide library books to the men who lived and worked for weeks in isolation in the lighthouses around Britain's shores.

These are only three of many, and all this was done in Elizabeth's spare time. First of all, she was a wife and mother, no matter how much she believed she was a poor example of one. She was also a minister in the Quaker faith. And as she believed her mission in life was to bring God's word and his love to as many as possible, it wasn't only in the Meeting Houses where she preached. There were the prisons too, and she travelled all over the country to do this work. There were Quarterly and General Meetings to attend. The convict ships needed visiting for inspection. And don't forget, she was never feeling very well at any time in her life. She suffered from nerves, fevers, faintness, exhaustion and travel sickness.

Her older children were marrying and leaving home. Elderly relatives and her own brothers and sisters were experiencing illness and death. Elizabeth was always there to help.

The unexpected death of her dearest sister, Rachel, at forty-nine came as a terrible shock. They had been so close during their childhood, and Elizabeth always felt Rachel was her superior and a much worthier person than herself. It was only the amount of hard work which faced her that kept her from collapsing in her grief.

There was always the worry over her husband's spending too. Wealthy though they were, she knew he spent far more than was wise. He could never resist valuable antiques or paintings. And he gave his children such lavish weddings that his own strict Quaker Fry relatives frowned upon him. To Joseph, giving these magnificent receptions was a show of love to his children. To his wife they were the cause of many sleepless nights.

Her own brothers and brothers-in-law were always trying to advise Joseph on business matters. Over the years, if ever it showed signs of running into difficulty, they would put a lot of money into his bank to keep him from trouble.

But Joseph Gurney suspected there would come a time when his sister would be faced with more financial problems than her family would be able or willing to help with. In his letters he began advising her to cut down on her vigorous life style and spend more time at Plashet House 'out of the public eye'. Elizabeth always assumed this was merely concern for her health. But it wasn't, not always.

Her brother knew that if the Frys fell into great financial trouble, her critics would rise up against her. Without the Fry wealth behind her, she would lose all the power and influence she had with officials and authorities.

Joseph Gurney was right to have these fears. In the late summer of 1828, when Elizabeth was forty-eight, she was going to embark on a very long tour in the north of England. It was one of the rare occasions when her husband went with her. It was a bad time to neglect his business but he wanted so much to be with Elizabeth.

There was nothing he liked more than to hear her crystal clear voice preaching passages from the Bible to the wide-eyed, entranced prisoners seated around her. Goodness shone out of her and lit up their drab surroundings. He loved to see how everyone welcomed his wife with open arms and warm hearts wherever she went to bring the word of God to their ears.

Two of the places they visited were Liverpool and York. Then they spent some free time in the Lake District for a rest before returning home. They were away for three months and it was a very successful tour. But sadness was awaiting their return in November. Business matters had gone very wrong.

Elizabeth's family helped by sending money to help them with their domestic and personal expenses. But they were no longer willing to risk investing money in Joseph's bank as they too could have ended up in the same situation.

By the end of November the Frys had lost all their money, and most of their possessions were taken away to pay their creditors. They were forced to sell Plashet House, the home they'd loved so much, and, for a time, Joseph and Elizabeth were in a daze. They couldn't believe it had all happened – and so quickly.

It didn't occur to them that there was worse to come. Anyone else in their situation would have received all the sympathy they could have given. But there were many who gave the Frys none at all.

There were always those who would leap at any chance to discredit the Society of Friends. Both Elizabeth and Joseph realised what harm their business collapse could do to it. Quakers were known for their honesty – their trustworthiness. Yet here was Joseph Fry, a Quaker banker, who had lost all his investors' money.

They didn't know how the Friends themselves would react to them. Would they accept them in their midst? Nothing could keep Elizabeth from going to the Meeting the following Sunday. She walked into the Meeting House and took her place in the gallery with the other elders.

How surprised they were when, after a few minutes of the silence, Mrs Fry slowly got to her feet. She looked weary and through the tears brimming in her eyes she gazed about her for a moment. Then they heard her sweet voice. Although trembling with emotion, her words could be heard throughout the building as she said, 'Though He slay me yet will I trust in Him.' She went on declaring her love and faith in God. No matter what had befallen her family, her trust in Him was unshaken.

Elizabeth was sure the Lord was punishing her for doing so little for him. She simply didn't want her family or the Friends to suffer because of her sinful ways. The Friends were reduced to tears with her. When the Meeting was over they came forward to offer their sympathy and support.

But how cruel her critics were. All over the country lies were being spread about Mrs Fry, the lady they would have given anything to be presented to just a matter of days earlier. She was accused of ruining her husband's business by taking money from his bank to give to the Newgate prisoners and to her other charities.

Not even the Gurneys were spared in the scandalous lies. Their good name was sneered at along with the reputation of the Society of Friends. They were pointed at and called ungodly. No Quaker was to be trusted.

It hurt Elizabeth enough to have these accusations made against her. But to include the innocent Friends and her family was unforgivable. Still, Elizabeth Fry was not an unforgiving woman. How she prayed to the Lord that no harm should come to others through her wickedness. And how the Lord must have smiled on her. God knew the truth and so did the evil-minded people who cast the slurs on her. They'd simply been waiting for an excuse to find some fault in a woman who was doing so much to help others.

One reverend gentleman said, 'We long to burn her alive for her goodness.'

Far from the Gurney family being angry at being brought into such a scandal, all their anger was directed against 'Betsy's accusers'. They came racing to the Frys' rescue. Joseph was given employment in one of their businesses. He would receive a good portion of his salary for his own personal use, but his wife would be given the main sum. It must have been a humiliating experience for Joseph Fry, but as Elizabeth was better at handling money than he was, he admitted it was the sensible thing to do.

With Plashet House lost to them, it meant they would have to live permanently at Mildreds Court. Elizabeth's young brother, Samuel, knew this would be quite unsuitable for them. He lived in a splendid mansion in the London suburb of West Ham. He also owned The Cedars, a house next door to his own, and he offered to rent it to them. It was much smaller than either Plashet House or Mildreds Court. But it was a lovely Queen Anne house with beautiful gardens surrounded by trees from which it got its name.

A few months after their financial disaster, Joseph Gurney asked his sister to go with him on another prison tour. And, to her surprise, whenever they made a stop anywhere, people she had known for years – sometimes all her life – refused to take Elizabeth into their homes. Prison governors turned against her too, and she was very upset at this change in people who'd had nothing but praise for her in the recent past.

Aged fifty, with the rapid change in her circumstances, Elizabeth Fry was feeling older than her years and a great depression came over her. She prayed to the Lord not to let her lose faith in humanity. It wasn't the loss of wealth which bothered her. It was the lack of faith and understanding in others that bewildered and saddened her.

She was called to appear before all sorts of committees to defend her actions in the past. When she was being questioned by these people, Elizabeth always made it clear that she sincerely believed she was doing God's work. Anyone opposing her was defying the Lord's wishes.

For this claim she was mocked and scorned by her interrogators. They laughed when she said, 'If prisoners were treated as human beings instead of animals, they would turn their thoughts towards God and away from wrongdoing.'

The authorities said, 'The more painful the punishment, the better.' They told Elizabeth her work had all been a waste of time. The prisoners only pretended to be influenced by her and God. As examples they used the very worst of criminals to prove their point.

Elizabeth was aware that some prisoners really were wicked and criminal. But she also knew there weren't many like that.

One committee was opposed to Mrs Brown's little shop in Newgate. They said it was responsible for much evil. Such luxuries only encouraged people to commit crime just to get into prison.

She was accused of making prisons too clean and comfortable. Sewing and knitting were just pleasant pastimes for women, not work, and certainly not punishment.

They accused Elizabeth of showing off by inviting her friends and relatives to the prisons to see and hear her reading to the prisoners and praying with them.

Elizabeth defended herself by saying the only reason they had been invited was to see what worthwhile work it was and the progress being made. As for her 'friends and family', they had distorted the truth. These were the Quaker Friends and many were her family.

Slavery in Britain had been abolished in 1811, largely through the efforts of William Wilberforce, one of Elizabeth Fry's greatest admirers. Many corrupt people were angry at the abolition. All Quakers were in favour of it because they detested slavery above all things, except perhaps war.

Now there was a move to have it abolished in every British colony in the world. And it was Elizabeth's brother-in-law, Fowell Buxton, who was leading the campaign.

Although she was wholeheartedly behind him in this, Elizabeth never became involved in the anti-slavery Act being presented to Parliament. But she was still accused of being involved in it.

Strangely, although she always believed she was failing in her duty to God and to her family, all this opposition seemed to give her an added strength. Maybe it was some remaining defiance lying hidden from the days when young Betsy Gurney revelled in standing up to opposition. Her faith in her work and, above all, in the Lord, kept her from retiring to the quiet life her critics would have sentenced her to.

With her brother she continued to carry out the tours, going only to the places where she was welcome, and there were still many, Newgate being one of them. But there was a new set of prison inspectors now who began to change everything back to the way it was. Cruelty was back in the prisons and, in most cases, Elizabeth and her Friends were unable to do anything about it.

The year before, Robert Peel had at last, after years of planning, established the first police force in Britain and it was a big success. The crime rate dropped rapidly because the police were solving more crime, which meant far more real criminals were being caught. Of course, this resulted in prisons being more overcrowded than ever. That was blamed on Elizabeth as well.

She only saw it as being presented with many more souls to save.

11: Seal of Approval

It was the letters from many well wishers that told Elizabeth the Lord was with her. They were the proof that more people supported her than were against her.

Letters came from William Wilberforce and his family, and from the Earl and Countess of Derby at Knowsley Hall where she'd been made so welcome. Was it really so long, she wondered, since that day when she'd prayed God's forgiveness for enjoying her stay there? There were letters, too, from her dear girlhood friend, the Duke of Gloucester and his Duchess. It seemed a lifetime since, as Prince William Frederick, he'd spent all those happy hours with the young Gurneys at Earlham Hall.

From all over Europe came support for Mrs Fry, and when her sad news reached Australia, people wrote from there too. Gradually her critics were overcome by her admirers' faith in her. Even without the wealth she'd once known, Elizabeth was keeping up her charitable work. No one could now accuse her of robbing her husband's bank to do it. There was no bank.

The letters praising the book she and her brother had written had always carried invitations for her to visit all the European countries. She began by going to Ireland and then the Channel Islands. Later she went over to the continent.

Despite everything that had happened, Mrs Fry was as popular as ever. It saddened her, though, to be in a situation in which she was able to give more advice and help in foreign countries than she was allowed to give in her own.

But then, in the summer of 1837, when Elizabeth was fifty-seven, a great change came over Britain.

King William IV died. He had no living children and his successor to the throne was his eighteen-year-old niece, Victoria.

Right from the beginning it was clear that the new Queen was a strong-minded woman. Men heeded what she said, thought and commanded. It was no longer wise to mock such people as Elizabeth Fry. Not when the whole of the British Empire, nearly half the world, was ruled by a woman – and one so very young.

Victoria was a great reformer. She firmly believed in improved conditions in prisons, asylums, hospitals, factories, mills, mines and workhouses. It took most of her sixty years' reign to achieve all she wanted for her subjects. But from her first coming to the throne, everyone could see that the change had started.

Someone the Queen admired almost above all others was Elizabeth Fry. She had earned the nation's esteem for the work she had been able to do outside her family commitments in such a day and age. Remember, women had few rights of their own and were more or less the property of their fathers and husbands.

The week before her marriage to Prince Albert, the Queen sent a Royal Command for Mrs Fry to go to see her. In the past, Elizabeth had met Queen Charlotte and later she had met the late King William's Queen, Adelaide. But those queens were merely kings' consorts. Victoria was the sovereign in her own right and it was the greatest honour anyone could know to be asked to see her. After this great honour, whenever Elizabeth returned to the continent, she was commanded by all the European

117

royal families to appear at their courts too.

Mrs Fry was now an elderly lady of ample figure. Still, the sweetness of her voice, her fine, flawless skin and shining eyes were like those of an eager young girl. Even the gold of her hair was unchanged.

The court appearances were such wonderful occasions that her Plain Quaker conscience was never at rest. She struggled but never managed to quell the guilt she felt for her love of royalty and grandeur.

She would tell herself she was doing God's work among Christian people. That the highest nobles in the land sought her company was nothing to be ashamed of. They were simply showing their approval of her doing her godly duties.

When she was a rather frail, elderly lady she had one of her greatest achievements: the order of Elizabeth Fry nurses was founded.

Up to that time, like the old prison turnkeys, nurses were drawn from the lowest ranks of human society. Drunken, vulgar women were the only people hospitals could get to do the many unpleasant tasks. They had no training, were dirty and neglectful and were probably responsible for more infections and deaths among their patients than if these unfortunates hadn't been taken into hospital at all. Hospitals themselves were as dirty as any prison. Sick and injured people would fight to exhaustion to avoid being taken off to such terrifying places.

Elizabeth's nurses were to be clean, sober and respectable religious women. They would wear a uniform, be given proper training and be paid a wage.

A while after this nursing order was founded a young woman went to see Mrs Fry to say how much she admired her and to praise her for what she'd done with the nurses. The girl herself had always wanted to nurse but her family had forbidden her to. It would have been disgraceful for a young lady from a respectable background to take up such an occupation because nurses had such a dreadful reputation. Well-brought-up girls weren't expected to go out to work. But there were many who, although rich enough not to have to earn their living, wanted to work for God and for mankind.

The young lady who went to see Elizabeth was just such a person. Her name was Florence Nightingale. Later, when she went out to Scutari to nurse the wounded from the Crimean War, it was a group of Elizabeth Fry's nurses that she took with her.

In her final years Elizabeth spent a lot of time with the nobility and royalty of every land. With her own high-born background she was able to associate with them freely. With their help she was able to carry on her work for the poor, the sick and the persecuted.

Yet she was always questioning herself, and most of the time felt a hypocrite rather than a good Quaker. How could she, a humble servant of God, justify her love of earthly majesty? Why did she like to be the centre of attraction? Why did she experience such delight when going to receptions and audiences at Windsor Castle, Buckingham Palace or the Mansion House, official residence of London's Lord Mayor?

She prayed and prayed for the Lord to keep her from her sinning ways. A Quaker should shun all the publicity and acclaim she received when being seen riding with these great people in their crested and gilded coaches.

Dancing and music were never indulged in nor did she ever stray from the simple Quaker dress. All the same she was always attracted to the beautiful clothes her non-Quaker daughters bought, and often accompanied them on their shopping expeditions.

119

Nearly all the Gurneys had married 'out' and most of the Fry children were following in their way. First there was Rachel's Anglican marriage. Then, one by one, her other offspring were being either baptised or marrying 'out', and Elizabeth respected their different beliefs. George Fox had said that people should be free to worship God in any way they thought best.

When her eldest son, John, married 'out', Elizabeth gave the marriage her blessing and he and his wife went to live at Mildreds Court. But when he bought a piano and installed it there, his mother nearly disowned him.

There was a time when her eldest daughter, Kate, nearly disowned her mother out of embarrassment.

King Frederick of Prussia was due to come to England to attend Queen Victoria's and Prince Albert's eldest child's christening. He had met Elizabeth on previous occasions in his own country and the two had become firm friends. As he was to be in England, he asked if she would take him to see Newgate, the prison which had become a model for all prison reformers.

Not only did Elizabeth agree, she also invited him to go to her home afterwards for luncheon.

Kate was horrified. 'How could you possibly ask a king to come here?' she said.

Elizabeth was disgusted that Kate should be ashamed of their humble little home. Kate thought that possibly Earlham Hall or Plashet House would have been suitable – but The Cedars in West Ham? Her mother accused her of 'pride and vanity at being ashamed of their little house' – although it was rather grand and not all that little. All the Frys and Gurneys she could collect were invited to the luncheon. The house was thoroughly cleaned and flowers adorned every room.

At Newgate, during the inspection, all the prisoners were

on their best behaviour. They sat quietly sewing while Elizabeth read a short piece from the Bible. Then everyone, including the royal party, knelt in prayer and it was noted that King Frederick had tears in his eyes.

At the end of the visit, the party got into the line of carriages and made their way to West Ham. Already Elizabeth was beginning to have doubts. Had she been as foolish as her daughter thought to invite the king? Whatever would her critics say of her? King Frederick was a very dear friend and there was nothing wrong in asking a very dear friend to ones home for luncheon. This she kept repeating to herself all the way home.

She was aghast – but secretly delighted – on approaching the roads near The Cedars to see the police out controlling the horse traffic. What an impressive sight it was as crowds lined the street and children cheered and waved as they passed.

The luncheon was most enjoyable, with the king asking for second helpings. Afterwards, Elizabeth held a silence and the king liked the guests so much that he stayed much longer than anyone expected.

All her family were enchanted by him, and his visit to her 'humble little home' did more to ease Elizabeth's conscience than anything had in the past. God's children came in all guises. There was no sin in a true Quaker befriending a good and honest man who cared only for those in his charge. That he just happened to be a king was a coincidence.

Nevertheless, the strain that led up to that luncheon made her so ill that she had to go away for a few days to rest and recover.

A tour of France was being planned for the following year and her family was worried. At sixty-three her lifetime's hard work was beginning to take its toll. She was showing much weakness in her limbs but nothing would convince her she had done all the Lord would expect from her. Off she went to tour as many French prisons, lunatic asylums and even hospitals as she could.

It was the last of Mrs Fry's European journeys. When she arrived home she admitted that her family was right. It was time to retire from so much work. She would simply carry on with her charity work at home and visit the prisons close by and the convict ships, but nothing more. Even then if any relative or friend was in trouble, she was there to help them.

Arthritis was getting a painful hold on her and she was barely able to hold a pen or a book. Soon she was finding difficulty in walking up and down the stairs and, shortly after, she was unable to walk at all. This was a bitter blow to a lady who had been so active, and she didn't take kindly to a wheelchair at first.

Her son, William, whom everyone knew was her favourite – although she tried not to show it – bought a house for her at Walmer, a picturesque fishing village in Kent. There, she and his father, with Kate, must settle down to have a long holiday, he said.

But his mother couldn't settle down. Unable as she was to walk, Walmer was a bit too isolated and cut off from the world for her. Still, she wouldn't hurt her son's feelings by saying so. She didn't have to. Within a month of her going there, scarlet fever swept through William's own home. His wife, children and servants survived, but William and a daughter died.

No one expected Elizabeth to survive this terrible grief. But she rallied. Indeed, she seemed to regain some of her old strength. It was as though God was easing her along in her sorrow. But within weeks, both Samuel Hoare and Fowell Buxton had died too.

That summer Elizabeth had a longing to return to Earlham, the childhood home of so many memories. It was as if she could see the end of her life drawing near.

When they were at Earlham, to everyone's surprise, in spite of her frail condition, she wanted to be taken to the Meeting House in Norwich.

What must have passed through her mind that Sunday morning? No longer the sulky, rebellious Betsy Gurney, 'mumping' at its being 'dis'. No longer a beautiful, slim young girl riding on horseback through the city, striving to quell the pride welling up in her from the admiring glances she received.

Plump, aged, golden hair faded to white, she rode through the city in a carriage. At Goats Lane Meeting House she was helped into her cumbersome wheelchair to be pushed through the Meeting House doorway. Even in her frailty, she held herself with dignity and her admirers were much greater in number than in her youth.

From her chair she spoke during the silence. Her feeble voice was steady and her words echoed round the low building. With each word there was added strength carrying her love for God to every corner of the building and into every heart.

In her prayers she begged the Lord to forgive her all her womanly vanities and weaknesses. No one present could have believed she had any.

The visit was Elizabeth's way of saying goodbye to Norwich and her lovely old home.

Later that year, as the summer was nearing its close, Joseph and Kate took her to Ramsgate in Kent. For the first time they saw her completely relaxed and at peace with herself as though resigned to await the Lord's calling her. All the family came to see them and she spent much of her time playing with her many grandchildren.

But there was something on her mind. Joseph was three years older than she was and she was desperately worried over what would become of him if she died and left him. But Joseph's children loved him so much that they assured her she had no need to worry. No doubt, Elizabeth felt that by dying and leaving her husband, she was committing another of her many sins.

It is a pity Elizabeth Fry could never believe in her own goodness. And yet, believing herself to be a sinner, she drove herself on and on right through her life to try to make up for her sins. Because of this, the world is indebted to her for the help she brought to other sinners all over the world.

When the end came it was quite sudden. She had a seizure from which she never regained consciousness.

Without ceremony, Mrs Fry, the once mischievous, ailing, confused Betsy Gurney was laid to rest in an unmarked grave in a Quaker burial ground at Barking, Essex, not too far from Plashet House.

It was October 1845, a day of rain and sharp winds, but more than a thousand people went to pay silent homage to the great lady.

As news of her death was spread abroad, millions the world over offered up prayers in gratitude to God for sending them such a dear and dedicated servant, one who gave Light to the Blind, Speech to the Dumb and Feet to the Lame.

At the greatest Royal Court of all, Elizabeth Fry had gained her place in the Kingdom of Heaven.

THE KINGDOM FACTOR

Roger Mitchell

We are living in extraordinary days. The rains of revival are on the way. The cloud is already bigger than a man's hand. All over the world is a resurgence of living Christianity. The coming in of the Kingdom of God in our generation is a real possibility. Whether or not this movement of God's spirit will finally bring the return of Jesus and the universal Kingdom of God will depend on the size of our vision of Jesus, the depth of our fellowship together in the Holy Spirit and the success of our evangelism. This can be the generation.

This is the thrust of evangelist Roger Mitchell's powerful book challenging Christians to bring in the Kingdom of God and to proclaim to a world desperately seeking answers that it is not some vague future hope, but a solid present.

WHEN YOU PRAY

Reginald East

Spiritual renewal has awakened in many Christians a deeper longing to know God more intimately. Prayer is the place where we personally meet God, yet it is often treated simply as the means for making requests for our needs, and offering our stilted, dutiful thanks. In this practical guide to prayer, Reginald East shows how we can establish a prayer relationship with God which is both spiritually and emotionally satisfying. Through understanding God and ourselves better, prayer can truly become an encounter with God, where we relax into Him, enjoy Him, listen as well as talk to Him and adventure into discovering His heart of love.

MY FAITH

Compiler: Mary Elizabeth Callen

Well-known Christians invite us in through their private doors to reveal fascinating glimpses of their most personal thoughts and deepest convictions about their faith.

The late Laura Ashley and her husband frequently turned to the Bible for advice on her growing business. Botanist David Bellamy knows who to thank for all he enjoys in life. At 102, Catherine Bramwell-Booth still lives to spread the message of Christ. Lord (Len) Murray found God in the poverty of London's East End. The presence of Christ transformed the agony of torture into 'a privilege' for Dr Sheila Cassidy. For Anne Watson, God became more real and more mysterious during her husband David's illness and death.

Their moments of peace, doubt, anger and pure joy are common to us all, yet their experiences confirm the uniqueness of God's love for each individual.

FORGIVE AND RESTORE

Don Baker

When a member of God's family, in this case a loved pastor, goes seriously off the rails in his personal life, the question looms large, 'What should the Church do about it?' 'Is it a matter for the church leadership only?' Should the wayward member be asked to leave or just relieved of responsibility? What should the congregation be told?

This book is a remarkable account of how one church dealt with such a highly charged and emotional crisis. It records in honest detail the ebb and flow of hope and despair, uncertainty and humanity, and relying throughout on biblical principles, it picks its way through a tangled mess to find a place of healing and restoration again.

ROCKING THE BOAT

William Davies

One outstanding feature of today's church is the rapid – even sensational growth of the House Church movement. Its supporters believe that they have come closest to establishing the Kingdom of God on earth, yet many Christians are far from happy with these claims.

This book aims to dispel the clouds of controversy which obscure a clear view of what the House Church is, how it operates, what are its main teachings and goals, and to encourage a deeper understanding and respect between the denominations and the House Church based on a humble willingness to learn from one another.

'. . . definitely the number one book so far on the strengths and weaknesses of the fastest growing Christian movement in this country.'

Michael Green writing in the *Church Times*

If you wish to receive *regular information* about *new books*, please send your name and address to:

London Bible Warehouse
PO Box 123
Basingstoke
Hants RG23 7NL

Name _____

Address _____

_____

_____

_____

I am especially interested in:

- [ ] Biographies
- [ ] Fiction
- [ ] Christian living
- [ ] Issue related books
- [ ] Academic books
- [ ] Bible study aids
- [ ] Children's books
- [ ] Music
- [ ] Other subjects

P.S. If you have ideas for new Christian Books or other products, please write to us too!